Dogs are
SMARTER than JACK

91 amazing true dog stories

Connecting animal lovers and helping animals worldwide

The publisher
Smarter than Jack Limited (a subsidiary of Avocado Press Limited)
New Zealand: PO Box 27003, Wellington
Canada: PO Box 819, Tottenham, Ontario, L0G 1W0
Australia: PO Box 170, Ferntree Gully, Victoria, 3156
www.smarterthanjack.com

The creators
SMARTER than JACK series concept and creation: Jenny Campbell
Compiler and typesetting: Lisa Richardson
Administration: Anthea Kirk
Cover design: DNA Design, Simon Cosgrove and Lisa Richardson
Cover photograph: © James Walshe. All rights reserved.
Story typing and editing: Patricia Reesby
Story selection: Jenny Campbell, Lisa Richardson, Lydia Crysell and others
Proofreading: Vicki Andrews (Animal Welfare in Print)
North American office: Eric Adriaans

The book trade distributors
United Kingdom: Airlift Book Company
Canada: Publishers Group Canada
United States: Publishers Group West
Australia: Bookwise International
New Zealand: Addenda Publishing

The participating animal welfare charities
The participation of the wonderful team at Dogs Trust is gratefully acknowledged. This book can be purchased through Dogs Trust, and through a number of other participating animal welfare charities. Please see the list on pages 146-148.

In the United Kingdom £3.00 from every sale made through Dogs Trust and 10p from every bookshop sale of this book will be donated to Dogs Trust. Dogs Trust was not responsible for the production, design or distribution of this book.

The legal details
First published 2005
ISBN 0-9582571-7-5
SMARTER than JACK is a trademark of Avocado Press Limited
Copyright © 2005 Avocado Press Limited

Contents

Responsible animal care

The stories in this book have been carefully reviewed to ensure that they do not promote the mistreatment of animals in any way.

It is important to note, however, that animal care practices can vary substantially from country to country, and often depend on factors such as climate, population density, predators, disease control, local by-laws and social norms. Animal care practices can also change considerably over time; in some instances, practices considered perfectly acceptable many years ago are now considered unacceptable.

Therefore, some of the stories in this book may involve animals in situations that are not normally acceptable in your community. We strongly advise that you consult with your local animal welfare charity if you are in any way unsure about the best way to care for animals in your community.

You may also find, when reading these stories, that you can learn from other people's (often unfortunate) mistakes. For example, if you have a dog it is important to make sure that it is appropriately and safely secured when you are not at home, and under close control in public places. Water can be a hazard too; if you have a swimming pool check that it is adequately fenced, and always keep your dog secure while at the marina! Cars are another potential danger; ideally you should not leave your dog alone in a car, but if this is unavoidable, make sure there is adequate ventilation and that it is only for a very short time.

We also advise that you take care to ensure your pet does not eat poisonous plants or other dangerous substances, and do not give any animal alcohol. In some rather extreme cases, you may even need to monitor what television channels your pet watches!

Creating your SMARTER than JACK

Dogs are SMARTER than JACK is a heart-warming book of tales about truly smart dogs. This is the first edition in the SMARTER than JACK series that is dedicated solely to dogs.

Many talented and generous people have had a hand in the creation of this book. This includes everyone who submitted a story, and especially those who had a story selected as this provided the content for this inspiring book. The people who gave us constructive feedback on earlier books and cover design, and those who participated in our research, helped us make this book even better.

The team at Dogs Trust assisted us greatly and were wonderful to work with. Profit from sales of this book in the United Kingdom will help Dogs Trust, and profit from sales of this book in other countries will help many other animal welfare charities, in their admirable quest to improve animal welfare.

Emma Milne wrote the thought-provoking foreword, Lisa Richardson compiled the stories, did the typesetting and helped with the cover design, James Walshe provided the beautiful cover photograph, Pat Reesby typed and edited stories, Anthea Kirk helped coordinate all the entries, Vicki Andrews did the proofreading, and many others helped with the enormous task of selecting and typing the stories.

Thanks to bookstores for making this book widely available to our readers, and thanks to readers for purchasing this book and for enjoying it and for giving it to others as gifts.

Lastly, I cannot forget my endearing companion Ford the cat. Ford is now 12 years old and has been by my side all the way through the inspiring SMARTER than JACK journey.

We hope you enjoy **Dogs are SMARTER than JACK** – and we hope that many animals and people benefit from it.

Jenny Campbell
Creator of SMARTER than JACK

Connecting animal lovers worldwide

Our readers and story contributors love to share their experiences and adventures with other like-minded people. So to help them along we've added a few new features to our books.

You can now write direct to many of the contributors about your experiences with the animals in your life. Some contributors have included their contact details with their story. If an email address is given and you don't have access to the internet, just write a letter and send it via us and we'll be happy to send it on.

We also welcome your letters for our 'Your say' section. These could be about animals in your life or about people who are out there making a difference.

Do you have an unusual question that other readers may be able to help answer? Some readers have posed a number of interesting questions, scattered throughout this book. Can you answer them?

Do you like to write to friends and family by mail? In the back of this book we've included some special SMARTER than JACK story postcards. Why not keep in touch and spread the smart animal word at the same time.

Since 2002 the popular SMARTER than JACK series has helped raise over NZ$280,000 for animal welfare charities. It is now helping animals in Canada, the United States, Australia, New Zealand and the United Kingdom.

The future of the SMARTER than JACK series holds a number of exciting books – there will be ones about cheeky animals, heroic animals and intuitive animals. You can subscribe to the series now too; more information can be found in the back of this book.

If you've had an amazing encounter with a smart animal we'd love to read about it. You may also like to sign up to receive the Story of the Week for a bit of inspiration – visit www.smarterthanjack.com.

The enchanting cover photo

Lucy, from Australia, is a five-year-old Rhodesian ridgeback who found herself at the RSPCA at the tender age of 12 weeks. Being left alone all day, Lucy was fretting, lonely and in need of companionship.

She has found a loving new home with lots of attention, walks and training. She is now very obedient and can even do a few tricks.

Rhodesian ridgebacks are one of the larger dog breeds so Lucy is very active and she needed someone who could give her lots of exercise and room to move.

In her new home she is well socialised and has fitted into her new family, giving total devotion, loyalty and love.

Lucy and lots of other RSPCA dogs can be found in the RSPCA's dog calendar. To order visit www.rspcavic.org.

The beautiful photograph of Lucy is by talented photographer James Walshe.

Foreword

Having been a qualified veterinary surgeon for nine years now I have encountered thousands and thousands of dogs, and their owners. With this catalogue of experience of the interactions between these two species, it would really come as no surprise to me if there was enough material for 100 books that highlight our inadequacies when compared to our canine companions!

I was thrust into the spotlight all those years ago too, and this has brought me into contact with many amazing canines that I never would have met in the course of my everyday work. Assistance dogs are some of the most amazing creatures you will ever come across. I have seen them turn off lights, load and unload washing machines, listen attentively to every word and even handle a pair of tights without laddering them. Let's face it; most men take decades of training to perform these tasks to even a rudimentary standard.

In the course of judging competitions for these friends of ours I have heard tales of unrelenting bravery, intelligence and loyalty. I have heard about dogs that can detect the scent of cancer in their human owners, predict when they are about to have a seizure and go for help without any training whatsoever. I have, on numerous occasions, caused looks of astonishment from my nearest and dearest as I have recounted one of these stories and sobbed all the way through it, just as I did when I was eight and I heard the theme music to *Lassie*.

My beloved mutts Pan and Badger (who, I hasten to add, get recognised about as often as I do, in their own right) are very placid beasts that I love with every cell in my body. They have come to work with me since they were puppies and have absorbed their training by some kind of osmosis that has made my life a very easy one. They know when they can run about like headless chickens (or Irish setters) and when they must behave at the surgery. I couldn't say for sure that they would run to a house and tell someone if I was trapped in a well but I can recall a time they were worth their weight in gold.

Emma Milne and friends

I was working in Cheltenham and lived near the college. I took 'the boys' for a last walk at about 11 o'clock. As I was heading home I could hear the approach of a small group of men behind me who sounded like they had supped one beer more than their verbal inhibitors could cope with. I knew they were probably nothing to worry about but they were a little unsettling and were gaining on me. I thought that the best plan of action was to step to one side, sit the dogs down and wait for them to pass so we didn't get to the point where we were walking together.

As the men drew level with me one of them leered over and made a growling noise towards us. About a third of a second later he realised this was a mistake as approximately 60 kilograms of hair and teeth launched across the pavement at him, puffed up to their maximum hackle size and emitting their most impressive and menacing bark. They didn't properly go for him; they just formed an impenetrable wall between me and them and made it very clear that the line was not one to be crossed. The whole group jumped in unison into the road and put both hands up, and then retreated down the road backwards like a gang of robbers that had been sprung with their hands in the till.

I, of course, acted nonchalantly as if I had known they would do this all along and called them to my side as the men retreated. Once they had gone I let the smile beam onto my face and gave them a whole load of praise. They had never done it before and they have not had reason to do it since, but I have no doubt now that they will sense how I feel and how someone else is acting and they will look after me to the best of their ability. I am a very proud 'mum'!

This may seem inconsequential and merely an act of instinct, but I think you will agree when you share in all these stories that perhaps it is us humans that really should be learning from our dogs. There certainly is room for a little more loyalty and selflessness in the world.

Emma Milne
Yorkshire
England

About Emma Milne

Emma Milne qualified as a vet from Bristol University in 1996. During her final year the BBC filmed the series *Vets' School*. After the success of this series she went on to be featured in *Vets in Practice*. It became very popular and ran for 11 series, including four Christmas specials.

Since being on *Vets in Practice*, Emma has appeared on numerous television programmes and has become well known for her forthright views on animal welfare issues. She currently works as a vet in Yorkshire and juggles this with her other work and the care of her beloved pets.

1

Smart dogs find solutions

A dog that can read?

Magnet, our blue merle koolie, runs down to the letter box each morning to collect the daily newspaper.

As we live on a battleaxe block, and the driveway is 100 metres long and hilly, it's a chore I am very happy for him to perform. But I can never send him for the paper on Wednesdays or Saturdays because of all the junk mail included with the paper.

Does Magnet read the 'No Junk Mail' notice?

Without fail, Magnet drops the paper, drags out the advertising inserts, leaving them on the ground, and heads back to the house with the paper. Obviously he can read the notice on our letter box saying 'No Junk Mail', which the delivery person can't.

Lorna Miller
Frenchs Forest, New South Wales
Australia

Write to me ... ✉
email Lorna at:
houndini@macexpert.net.au

Toby's stick

We took Toby, our ten-year-old rough collie, for a long walk to a local reservoir.

Between the car park and the gate, he picked up a stick to take with us. When he reached the gate he found that the stick, which was about one and a half metres long, was too wide to go through. After three tries he realised he wasn't going to be able to walk through the gate with the stick.

He stepped back a couple of metres and put the stick down on the ground so that it pointed vertically towards the gate. Then he picked up the stick at the end nearest to the gate and walked through, pulling the stick behind him. When he was two or three metres inside, he put the stick down, picked it up in the middle again and carried on his way.

Does this show that dogs can reason?

John and Janet Linton
Launceston, Cornwall
England

Toby the clever collie

Bless you!

Brillo, my Airedale terrier, was lying in front of the fire while my husband Alisdair and I were sitting at the dining room table, having our lunch.

Suddenly I sneezed. Brillo got up, went across to Alisdair, pulled a hanky out of his trouser pocket, walked around the table with it and gave it to me.

Adrienne Bradley
Milngavie, Glasgow
Scotland

Dusty and the 'stupid chicken'

I had a husky/German shepherd cross named Dusty. He was a wonderful dog and a devoted and loyal companion, but only to me.

At the time of this story, we had a 'short slab' fence across the front of our trailer. One afternoon when I returned home from work at the post office, some of my chickens had ventured beyond the fence and were scratching around in the dirt on the driveway. As I turned off the road I had to stop to avoid hitting them.

Old Dusty came out and surveyed the scene. He looked at me sitting there and looked at the chickens, who hadn't moved. Then he proceeded to herd them out of the way. They all scurried around the fence and headed for the backyard – that is, all but one. This one seemed to think she could get home the short way, through a small opening between the slabs. However, only her head would fit through the opening so she just sat there.

Again, Dusty looked at me and at the chicken. He nudged her a couple of times but she kept trying to go through the hole that was not big enough to fit more than her head. Finally, Dusty had had enough of this 'stupid chicken' so he grabbed her by the tail feathers, pulled her back out of the hole and herded her around the fence and home. He looked at me, totally pleased with himself, as if to say, *See, I knew what to do!*

Rose-Anne Kirkeeng
Hudson's Hope, British Columbia
Canada

Donna was quick to learn

Donna was a 'rescue' dog, thrown out on the street when she was a puppy. By the time she was picked up she was trying to fend for herself in a busy town centre and was a pitiful sight.

Her early experiences made her streetwise and gave her an independent streak but she was bright and learned quickly. She learned both good and bad habits easily. When she was about eight months old and generally responding well to her recall command of 'Donna, come!' she happened upon a discarded bag of sandwiches. In seconds, her nose was into the bag; she gulped down a sandwich and ignored my call for her to come and also my command to 'leave'. She picked up the bag and ran up the field away from me, stopping to scoff another sandwich. I pursued her up and down the field while she carried her spoils far enough to eat a sandwich before picking up the bag and racing off again. The bag seemed bottomless and eventually she had eaten eight sandwiches. She then brought me the empty plastic bag with a wag of the tail.

She went on to a successful obedience career, reaching the highest class (Test C) and competing at Crufts in the inter-regional obedience competition in 1994, representing the Northern Team.

 5

Donna was smart and streetwise

She also reached the Bakers Rescue Dog finals that year. I am proud of her achievements, the more so because of the poor start she had in life. I had her for nearly 17 years.

Elaine Hunter
Darlington
England

Scamp decided it was time for bed

Time for bed

Scamp, my three-year-old Jack Russell terrier, sits close by as I empty the washing machine. He likes to snatch a sock and run off with it, but if I actually give him an old pair of socks he is simply not interested.

Last summer I put his bed outside to air on the front lawn as it was a very hot day. I spent the evening gardening and when it got to 9.30 pm, way past his bedtime, I looked around to see him dragging the blanket from his bed, right around the house to the open back door. He took it into the hallway and curled up on it.

Obviously he was so tired that he couldn't wait any longer for his bed to be brought in.

Ms P A Kent
Swindon, Wiltshire
England

Snoopy the hitchhiker

Snoopy, a cocker spaniel, was so named because of his similarity to the cartoon character, with a white body framed by black ears and tail and, what is more, startling wit and lively charm.

One Sunday morning when the church bells were calling the villagers to prayer, Snoopy was sniffing out trouble in our back garden. He would often loiter playfully around the house, chasing a tennis ball, chewing chunks of wood or relaxing, loose-limbed, in the garden. When I peeped through the window that morning, he was knee-deep in a colourful bouquet of daffodils. I suspected he was after a bee. Time passed into late morning and late morning into lunch, and then someone knocked on the door.

My mother frowned; she was about to serve lunch and I could see lines of irritation sift across her face. My father sat motionless in his chair – village life did not suit him. My brother stayed sitting, wide-eyed. I huffed and puffed with annoyance but nonetheless opened the door, which had sounded for a second time.

An elderly woman stood before me, one arm propped against the wall while the other hung long against her skirt.

'Do you have a dog?' she enquired.

'Yes.'

'Is he a cocker spaniel?'

'Yes.'

'Have you lost him?'

This was a surprise. 'No,' I firmly replied.

'Are you sure?'

'Quite sure, he's in the garden. I'll get him for you if you like.' I turned to do so, but she held me by the arm.

'Don't bother, because I think you'll find I've got him.'

She moved to where a red mini was parked in the drive. I twisted and craned my neck but all I could see was another woman in the passenger seat.

'Where?' I asked. And then I saw him. He was sitting in the back seat, staring out at me, with a vague grin on his face.

'How on earth did he get there?'

At this, the woman could no longer retain her serious expression and let slip a soft smile.

'We – my sister and I, that is – were driving along the road – the one which leads into town – when we spotted your dog, or rather he spotted us. He came out into the middle of the road and stood barking at our car, almost as if he wanted us to stop. I put the brakes on and opened up the door. He peered in and without a moment's hesitation sprang into the back seat. Of course we recognised him from the village and knew where you lived, and so here we are!'

'Thank goodness,' I said. He must have clambered up the bank of the garden, I thought, and scrabbled through people's gardens, to find himself in the main road.

I looked over the lady's shoulder. He was still sitting there, grinning – yes, he really could have been the larger-than-life version of the cartoon character. But what a clever dog, not only to avoid being

 9

run over, but to have the foresight to 'hail a cab' to get him home again. And what a choice of cab. Yes, a red mini was just his scene.

Georgina Lois Woolley
Dorchester, Dorset
England

Chloe figured out how to keep her banana peel and eat her dinner too!

Which should I eat first?

Chloe, my whippet, was about seven months old at the time. My mum had just thrown out some scraps, including a banana peel. Chloe took a fancy to it and spent the next couple of hours chewing what was left of the inside.

It was about 6 pm and time for her dinner. She followed me, the banana peel still in her mouth, to the spot on the veranda where her food bowl was usually kept. I put the bowl down, and then went inside to join my family at the dinner table.

I looked out the glass door to see if Chloe was into her tucker, only to find her in a bit of a dilemma. She didn't know whether to eat her banana peel before someone stole it, or whether she should leave the banana peel in case someone tried to steal the food from her dog bowl.

She moved her head from the banana peel to the dog bowl five times before she came to a decision. She picked up the banana peel, placed it right beside her bowl and put her paw on it. Only then did she start eating from her bowl. I was surprised at how quickly she was able to fix her tricky situation. In the end she was able to eat both meals.

Vanessa O'Connor
New South Wales
Australia

If you expect me to pay, I'll get the next tram

My aunt, who lived in Leeds 60 years ago, had a large white and tan dog called Tony.

There were no dog wardens in the 1940s, and much less traffic. No one thought it unusual for dogs to go out alone in city streets, if they wore a name tag. Tony made the rounds of neighbours and local shops, where people would offer him titbits.

His favourite haunt was the recreation ground where the local boys played football. He knew when it was time for them to come out of school, and he'd go and join in their games. The ground was a mile and a half away up a steep hill from his home, and as he grew older he found the walk home a little too much for his tired legs.

Following an entirely different route from the one he'd taken on foot to the playing field, he'd head for a nearby tram stop, jump aboard as soon as one going his way drew up, and ride in comfort back to his house.

Some conductors would make him get off, as dogs were supposed to pay a fee to travel. Undeterred, Tony simply waited for the next tram.

Kate Bunting
Mabelthorpe, Lincolnshire
England

I forgot to check under the bed

In 1966 I wrapped a Morris Minor around a lamp post, and instead of going back to my bedsit I spent the night with friends.

Hamish, their black Labrador, and I were great friends. The next day, when he came back from his walk, he rushed up to the spare room to see if I was still there.

On his way down, he suddenly stopped, went back up and looked *under* the bed – the one place he had forgotten to look. At least it shows that dogs think and reason.

M M Raymer
Corbridge, Northumberland
England

2

Smart dogs amaze us

My watch still worked

We had a little terrier mix that we took everywhere. We led active lives and Rocky loved to tag along.

One Sunday afternoon while we were fishing, the pin in my watch strap broke and my watch fell off. I couldn't find it anywhere, chalked it up to bad luck and thought nothing more of it.

Two weeks later we were fishing at the same pond close to where I'd lost my watch. Rocky was roaming round so I said casually, 'Go find my watch', laughing when she gave me a serious look. Five minutes later, she was at the edge of the water pawing at a rock about two inches under the water. She made a low barking sound and was determined to get at what she'd found.

Finally I bent down to see what she was digging at. To my amazement, there under a rock beneath the water was my watch. And it still worked.

Stephanie Coates
St John's, Newfoundland
Canada

Roc around the clock

Roc, a black Labrador, came to stay with me when his owner was away for several weeks. He and I knew each other from when I had visited his home.

There was just one problem. I had a clock which struck once on the hour. Roc seemed to think it was the doorbell, and he barked as if he expected me to answer it. I couldn't convince him that no response was needed.

Next time the clock struck, I went over and moved it on an hour. *Dong!* Roc listened, tilting his head. On again, and *Dong!* and a further tilt. This went on until I feared he'd get a dislocated neck. We returned to the fireside and he went to sleep.

In due course ... *Dong!* Awakened, he jumped up, barking, before a thought appeared to occur to him: *Oh, it's that thing again, I don't need to bark*. He lay down and went to sleep again. He had no further reaction to the clock throughout his visit.

M Leng
York
England

A tiny dog finds his way 'home'

Chester didn't look much like his mother, who was a cat-sized mixture of Maltese, poodle and chihuahua – a 'maltipoochi'. He was part of a litter fathered by a larger dog in the mobile home park where we lived in Madeira Park, British Columbia in 1975. My brother and his family adopted him as a puppy and took him to live in Powell River, 60 kilometres of highway plus a ferry ride north.

When he grew, his body wasn't much larger than his mother's but his legs were at least twice as long – a trait that would serve him well later in life. His muzzle had the whiskery look of an old man, but behind his somewhat comical-looking face was an intelligent brain and a happy, loving heart.

A few months after Chester was taken to Powell River, we had to give away his mother, Puppets, when she developed a jealous and potentially aggressive attitude towards our baby son who was just learning to crawl. Over the next few years, Chester occasionally came with my brother and his family from Powell River for short visits. He loved children and was always playful and full of energy.

In the spring of 1978 we moved from our mobile home into a new house six kilometres away and four kilometres off the highway down a narrow winding road. Shortly afterwards Chester visited for a few hours, but we didn't see him again until late that fall.

On a wet and chilly Sunday morning in November, I was enjoying a cup of coffee when I heard whining and scratching at the back door. I was dumbstruck to see Chester on the step, wet and shivering. I looked out to the driveway, expecting to see my brother's car, but no one was there. How on earth had Chester gotten there? That was a question that would go unanswered for the next two days.

I let Chester in; he was ravenously hungry. Because we had no dog at that time, we had no dog food, but Chester was too hungry to be fussy, and gobbled down any meat I could offer him. I phoned my brother's house in Powell River but there was no answer. In those days there were no answering machines or call display so I kept calling back all day, to no avail.

No one seemed to know where my brother and his family might be. There was nothing to do but make Chester feel at home and keep phoning back. I still had no clue as to why or how he'd arrived at our back door.

The following evening I learned the story of his journey. My brother and his family had left on Friday morning for Vancouver

 15

to spend the weekend looking for a new car. Besides the ferry from Powell River, a trip to Vancouver required a ferry ride from Langdale to Horseshoe Bay. Langdale was over 70 kilometres from our home in Madeira Park, and it was while my brother and his family were waiting at the terminal for the ferry that Chester ran off. They searched all over the terminal, calling his name, but there was no sign of him. They feared that someone in the terminal had let him into their car and 'dog-napped' him. When the ferry arrived they reluctantly boarded, thinking they would never see him again.

But as they would happily learn, Chester had not been dog-napped. We never learned what caused him to run away, but we do know that when he found himself alone at the ferry terminal his instincts kicked in and he decided to take matters into his own paws.

Over the next two wet and chilly days, this little dog managed to trot over 70 kilometres from the ferry terminal to our house. He had never been to the ferry terminal before and had been to our house only once, six months earlier.

His previous travelling had all been in a vehicle, so he had no chance to learn the scent of the route. Yet he was able to find his way through a maze of streets from the terminal back to the highway, and then follow the highway for 60 kilometres while ignoring all the possible turn-offs he could get lost on. Finally, he had to select the right turn-off that led to our house and ignore numerous side roads in order to arrive on our doorstep. Some people driving in cars – including me – would have a hard time doing that on the first attempt.

I've read about lost animals finding their way back home over long distances and even finding the new home after getting lost while the family was moving, but I am still amazed at this dog's sense of connection to us that enabled him to find our house. I can only assume that because he was born in our home, even though it wasn't the same house, he never lost the spiritual connection that guided him safely to our doorstep.

Dan Wiley
Terrace, British Columbia
Canada

Benjie reacted when there was a dog on television

Benjie leaped up when he heard the jingle

My family has kept dogs all through my 69 years of life, and all had their own personalities. Smaller breeds are easier for me to handle now, and I'm the delighted owner of two West Highland terriers. Bonnie is 11 and Jamie is four.

 17

Some years ago I offered to look after a neighbour's Westie while they were on holiday. The neighbour told me that Benjie would be no trouble at all – unless he saw a dog on television. If he did, he would dash over to the TV, bark like crazy and try to jump up and into the screen. I was told that Benjie even recognised the musical jingles that preceded any advertisement featuring a dog, and he'd react by diving off his chair and dashing to the television, even before the dog had appeared on the screen.

I was keen to see this, since most animal behaviourists and vets I'd spoken to had told me that dogs cannot see anything two-dimensional, which of course television is. I told my neighbour that my own Westie didn't react this way, and he said Benjie had only started when he was five.

Well, Benjie stayed with us for some weeks. During that time, he never missed a dog on television and he demonstrated that he recognised every musical jingle and was able to tell which piece of music would produce an advertisement where a dog would appear. It was fascinating to watch, especially since Bonnie, my Westie – who was four years old at the time – took no notice whatsoever of television. I was intrigued to find out whether she'd develop a similar interest when she turned five.

I can truthfully say that exactly the same thing happened. One day, when I thought she was sleeping, she dived off her chair and over to the television, where she barked furiously at a dog that had appeared. She became so excited that she jumped up, and her paw accidentally pressed the 'off' button and turned the set off.

She is now 11, knows all the jingles and quickly learns any new ones connected with dogs. She rushes over to the set, and even barks at cartoon drawings of dogs. You can see her head and eyes scanning the screen to wherever the dog happens to move next.

Since Jamie is now four, I'm waiting impatiently to see if he develops the same ability when he turns five. I saw David Attenborough on TV, discussing dolphins and saying they were the only animal able to see in two dimensions. Well, I know two Westies that can do the same. I even met a lady in the park who said she had a Westie who could see dogs on the television. She made her comment first; I hadn't mentioned my own experiences. I wonder if it's something peculiar to West Highland terriers. I've never experienced it with another breed of dog.

And I wonder why it takes until the age of five for this trait to manifest itself. I suppose it's something to do with the maturity of the brain and eye coordination.

Peggy Mullally
Leamington Spa, Warwickshire
England

Write to me ... ✉
Peggy Mullally
47 Leam Terrace
Leamington Spa
CV31 1BQ
United Kingdom

Cindy and Juli put their skills to good use

Cindy was my dream dog from the start.

She turned out to be the sort of collie – much less common than people imagine – who almost trains herself. Her talents led us to many challenges in the canine world, including competitive obedience and agility.

I think I was in danger of being mobbed by other competitors at one of her early shows. Cindy had already won rosettes in Beginners Obedience, Clear Round Jumping, Best Trick and Dog in Best Condition. The final class was for The Dog the Judge Would Most Like to Take Home. That judge was not very diplomatic. Instead of at least making a show of examining the other entries, he glanced around in a cursory way before asking, 'Now where's my little favourite?' and handing me that most coveted of red rosettes.

Cindy first learned her obedience 'stays' in front of a camera and took her duty as a photographer's model seriously. Her younger sister Juli, though similarly trained to stay still and pose for the camera, was more laid-back when facing a lens. Sometimes you might think, by her relaxed expression, that Juli had just cracked a rather vulgar joke, while, beside her, Cindy, upright and dignified, would be wearing her Queen Victoria 'We are not amused' look.

Agility competitions suited their active build and intelligence. In these competitions, the dogs race round a course of jumps and other obstacles without collar or lead. The starter says quietly, 'In your own time – go', and Cindy always recognised the word 'Go' although said by a stranger. Without waiting for my official command, she changed from a silent, steady dog to an enthusiastically speeding, barking maniac who jumped far higher than the two and a half foot obstacles. We had a flying start with her in command. Juli went one better, and on one course she cleared the high ring fence as well, both over and back when I recalled her. But they could also jump onto a five foot wall for fun, and balance there.

At the time puppy Juli joined us, Cindy's education had advanced to searching for hidden objects. She would sit obediently, quivering with anticipation, while Juli and I hid her favourite toy. Released, she would gallop to investigate where we had been. I was amused at how often the much younger Juli would give away the position of the toy by toddling towards it.

Searching proved useful. Both would race to find dog leads or other belongings I had dropped by mistake. They pointed out wild creatures in distress, like a starving young hedgehog, or a tiny sick rabbit that Cindy nosed and licked tenderly. Cindy was so gentle with my pet hamsters that we used to joke that she watched *Lassie* films on the quiet.

Once they acted like true heroines and possibly saved a pensioner's life. Roaming off on a narrow side path in the country, they found an old lady who had slipped and fallen and was hidden by high grass. They came rushing back to me, side by side as they so often travelled. The old lady was shaken and couldn't get up without my help. No one could have seen her from the main path. She had already lain there for some time and could have been stuck much longer, chilled by the wet grass.

It may have been just another search game for Cindy and Juli, but I felt extra proud of them, my splendid pair of talented sisters.

Louisa Maguire
Edinburgh
Scotland

Phenomenal sense of smell

Pax, my yellow Labrador, was a clever dog. Like most of her breed she was obedient, affectionate and incredibly greedy. As we strolled the country lanes, her greatest pride was to sniff out a discarded burger, cheese roll or ham sandwich and bring it to me, tail wagging in anticipation of an extra treat.

We live in an Essex village with about a thousand inhabitants. Once a year this swells to about 10,000 as we have a festival with sideshows, dog show and a ten kilometre road race. To add to the fun, there are tombola stalls, country dancing, bookstalls and a food tent filled with such goodies as bacon sandwiches, home-made cakes and other delicious foodstuffs made by the hard-working ladies of the Women's Institute. Creative arrangements of flowers fill every

 21

windowsill, nook and cranny of the stately Norman church, which has appeared in episodes of *Lovejoy* and on *Songs of Praise*.

On the Thursday night before this exciting weekend a large lorry, filled with flowers from Holland, rumbles through the narrow streets and stops outside the church. A band of women, carrying buckets, scissors and other florists' paraphernalia, descends on the lorry, hoping to collect the best blooms for their individual designs. Then the work begins.

I am one of those women and Pax, being a well-behaved elderly dog, would always go with me. One day, when we opened the big wooden doors, the fragrance of a lorryload of flowers was overwhelming. Pax sniffed the air and, ignoring everybody else, made her way to the back of the church and stood looking at me, wagging her tail. I followed her, as she knew I would, and there, at the end of the pew, against the twelfth century wall, was half a digestive biscuit.

Her sense of smell must have been phenomenal to sniff out a small biscuit among the thousands of different scents from all those exotic flowers. Armfuls of greenery had been gathered from the hedgerows, smelling strongly of the foxes, deer and other wild animals that live in the countryside.

Lesley Sinfield
Essex
England

Friday's card game means treats for Thomas

This is a tale that will show you what great memories dogs have.

Thomas is my eight-year-old Lowchen, a small dog with a big heart. He could be described as my baby in a fur coat.

Thomas worked out how many treats he should get each Friday

For over a year now I have enjoyed a game of cards with three friends every Friday evening. For the first few evenings they came, Thomas hardly stirred from his comfortable spot on the chair. Gradually he began to realise that he could use the situation to his advantage. With his big brown eyes and soulful expression he started systematically to work on my friends, and before long they were each bringing him a doggy treat every time they came over.

Very soon I noticed that, as soon as I prepared the table and the cards for our game, Thomas would immediately go and sit by the front door. Eventually one friend would arrive. Thomas would

 23

dutifully sit and receive his reward and then go straight back and sit by the door. This was repeated until my three friends had arrived. Then he would immediately return to his chair and allow us to enjoy our game of cards.

On a few occasions we would play a game with three rather than four players (meaning only two visitors). Thomas would sit for a long time patiently waiting by the door for the friend who was not playing that evening until I called him away. He would look accusingly at me and reluctantly return to his chair.

Now, you cannot tell me that Thomas doesn't remember the association of the cards and his treats or that he can't count!

Mary Delcourt
Ashby
Western Australia

Sandy the singing Shetland sheepdog

Our Shetland sheepdog Sandy would 'sing' whenever he heard music by Mozart.

Every day he would walk to our music centre and sit there until I put a Mozart tape on. He would then walk to one of the speakers and 'sing', with his head in the air. If I put on a tape which wasn't Mozart he would walk away. His favourite was the *Horn Concerto*, which I played so often the tape wore out.

We bought a record with short pieces by different composers. Music by Mozart would come through at intervals throughout the record, and Sandy would only 'sing' to the Mozart music.

We went to the Lake District on holiday and one day we were with Sandy in a shop where background music was being played. Mozart's *Eine Kleine Nachtmusik* came on and Sandy sat there singing throughout the piece. The shopkeeper said, 'Leave him in, it will attract customers.'

Sandy would follow me all over the house, even sitting in the bathroom when I had a bath. If I started to go upstairs he would go up ahead of me, turn to face me and walk upstairs backwards, putting his hind legs on the step behind him all the way up, just to make sure I was following.

He died a few years ago, and for a while afterwards I could not bear to listen to Mozart's music. It brought tears to my eyes.

Connie Pickard
Keighley, West Yorkshire
England

Stand still ... pheasant

It's amazing how many words a dog understands over the years. Try making a list sometime – you will be surprised.

I insist that wildlife and farm stock are left alone by saying, 'Leave – sheep' or 'Leave – pheasant'. The dogs soon understand. Tiffin is a blue merle collie, one of those who must be in front all the time, which is why our heel work has always been our downfall in obedience competitions. She runs ahead about 20 yards, comes back and then it's off ahead again.

One day, during one of our favourite walks near the river along a twisty narrow path, Tiffin disappeared around a bend. She didn't come back, and when I rounded the bend I saw she was standing still and looking back at me. As I got closer, I noticed movement by her legs. There were a dozen young pheasant chicks running round and through her legs. She just stood still, and soon all the chicks vanished into the undergrowth.

 25

I didn't see the hen pheasant who must have been leading the chicks, and I hadn't spoken a word. But Tiffin had automatically stopped still. She was only eight months old at the time, and was highly praised.

Mrs M J Goddard
Woodbridge, Suffolk
England

Tiffin knew to leave the pheasant chicks alone

That's not the right car

One rainy evening my father had to go into town to the store.

After he left, my mother's Belgian shepherd Tracker started barking and pawing at the front door. He appeared quite anxious, so my mother put on her shoes and went out to see what was wrong.

Tracker flew around the house. My mom kept asking what was wrong, as he was whining, barking and running up and down the driveway.

Mom said, 'Where's my car?' and he barked and ran in circles. I think he was alerting my mom that the car was gone. My father's car wasn't working; he doesn't usually take Mom's car and Tracker knew that.

Jennifer Carpenter
Fredericton, New Brunswick
Canada

She followed the route of the school bus

My husband Bob and I live in a mountainous ranching valley in the high country of southern British Columbia where we raise cattle and horses.

We have rivers, lakes, forests and alpine meadows. We also have an abundance of wildlife such as bear, moose and deer, and of course where the deer go, so do the cougars.

In the dozen years we have owned the ranch, our interactions with the valley wildlife have all been positive. We leave them alone and they leave us alone. At least that is how it was until November 2002.

Kip, our 12-year-old Australian shepherd, was my right hand and best friend, always just behind me. She was getting a little slower due to age, and arthritis had given her a slight limp that cut into her quality time of chasing marmots, but she still helped move the cattle and supervised everything on the ranch.

On a bitterly cold November day, my husband let her out of the house so she could lie at the top of the driveway, as she did every

 27

day, and wait for me to come home from work. But when I drove in there was no Kip to greet me, and a quick reconnaissance of the barnyard proved there was no dog there either. Bob and I called and hunted for her all over the property until it got dark, and then we took flashlights and combed our 360 acres to no avail.

We put signs up all over our small town with her picture and description, and contacted everyone in our area. Kip had never been more than 50 feet from us in the 12 years we'd had her.

After a sleepless night, with many trips to the front porch to see if she was there, we called our neighbour, an extremely good animal tracker and an experienced cougar hunter. It didn't take him long to find cougar tracks not more than 70 feet from our house and they clearly told the story of what had happened to Kip.

She had been at a paddock fence, probably barking at the horses, when the cougar, crouched down behind a stack of hay, took three big jumps and cornered her against the fence and the hay. All that was left of Kip were scuffle marks on the ground and some tufts of hair. Our neighbour said that in all likelihood the cougar had killed her instantly with a bite to the head, dragged her under the fence and taken her away.

We were devastated. For three days my husband and our neighbour scoured the mountain for any sign of the cougar and its kill. All they found were tracks, which was extremely rare due to the ground being well frozen and no snow down at that time. Our grief was huge but we still had to function. I went to work and my husband continued his job as a school bus driver in the area.

Eight days after Kip went missing we received a call from a friend who lives about eight miles away, on the other side of the mountain that we live behind. She said she thought she'd seen our dog in her cow field that afternoon. Before we could drive over to check, another call came in from the same area, saying they had also seen

Kip. We couldn't believe it was her, but did we hustle to drive over there! It was getting dusk and there was no sign of the dog, but enquiries to several other farms on that road convinced us that Kip – or a dog looking very much like her – had appeared in that area.

The last person we spoke to said the dog was travelling right up the middle of the road and moving like she had a purpose. In the pitch dark, cars were almost hitting her and at the last minute would swerve around her. She didn't waver from her course, which was right up the middle of the road. We walked the road for miles in the dark, calling her name, but our efforts proved futile and finally we had to call it a night.

The next morning I continued the search at daybreak while my husband went to do his morning school bus run. Imagine my joy when, after his run, he drove over to find me and to give me the incredible news that he had found Kip and she was at home.

As usual, he had picked up the kids along his regular route and had pulled in to the elementary school parking lot to let the youngsters off. He couldn't believe what he saw. There was Kip, lying on the sidewalk in front of the school. He just about ran over the kids in his rush to get out of the bus and go to her. She was weak, lame and very thin, but very glad to see him.

What was her story? The closest we can guess is that by some miracle she was quick enough to scramble under the fence and get in with the horses when the cougar cornered her. Perhaps the horses milling around disorientated the cougar just long enough for her to get away, or maybe a well-aimed kick from a horse discouraged her attacker. We will never know, but we do know that she must have run for a long time, probably become frightened again for some reason, and eventually lost her way. She lost a third of her body weight during the time she was gone.

Only Kip knows what happened during her amazing journey back to her family

All the sightings showed she was moving along the road in a westward direction. That road is the route that Bob takes with his school bus. That evening she must have travelled about ten miles to arrive at the elementary school. Kip had never been to that school or area in her life, and she was a dog who distrusted small children and would never place herself where they would be. But there she was, lying on the sidewalk in their midst and waiting for Bob.

We believe that in her travels she came across a scent that she recognised – Bob's school bus. She tracked that bus, right up the middle of the road, until it brought her to the first stop on his route, the elementary school. Then she lay down and waited. She knew he would eventually turn up; she had the scent to prove it.

Where Kip was for eight days, how far away and what she did to survive – that is her story and unfortunately she can't tell us. But what she has told us is that she truly is smarter than Jack.

Jill Hayward
Louis Creek, British Columbia
Canada

Did Spanky read the destination board?

When I was small, my parents had a dog called Spanky. Don't ask me why he had that name – unless it had something to do with his tail.

My parents owned a shop about two miles away, and one day Spanky followed my mother to the bus stop when she went to the shop. Of course she told him to go home, but when the bus arrived he walked round to the front and looked up at the destination board. My mother thought no more of it but, when she got to the shop,

 31

Spanky was sitting on the doorstep waiting for her. We always swore that dog could read.

On another occasion, my brother and I were at a local park when I fell in the lake. Being only two or three years old I couldn't swim, but Spanky jumped into the water and towed me to the side, where my brother pulled me out.

Spanky would never leave my side until I was safely inside our front gate.

Lorraine Bilton
Derby
England

Why did Henri go to Camber?

We lived on the edge of Kent, near Camber Sands and the town of Rye. Lydd was a wonderful place to bring up a family, and was fast becoming a very special place to us.

Henri, our Dalmatian, was always escaping from the house. One day I arrived home at 1.30 pm to find him gone, although we had a six foot fence all around our house, and a locked seven foot gate. I was always puzzled by his disappearances and thought of tying him up by a long chain but couldn't bring myself to tether him.

Later on that evening, Henri came home and I thought no more about it. The next day was Saturday and I did some local shopping. A friend approached me.

'Did you know I saw Henri getting off the bus from Camber yesterday?'

'Who was with him?' I asked.

'No one,' she said. 'He was his usual cheeky, prancing self.'

I telephoned the bus company later, to ask what had happened. I was told the driver had seen Henri get on but had thought he was with someone. The dog got off at the Camber bus stop. On the return journey, the bus driver noticed a Dalmatian waiting by the bus stop on the side of the road. Henri jumped on the bus and got off at the Lydd bus stop.

The driver wondered how he knew which stop to jump off at.

Patricia Rose Ribbits (née Sweeney)
Dymchurch, Kent
England

How does a magpie communicate with a dog?

I have quite a collection of pets – being an animal lover and all – but, out of them all, I have to say the strangest is my magpie Georgie. I also have two Jack Russells, Cleo and Minnie. One day we were kicking a ball around and Minnie looked like she bowled George over onto his back. George lay there squawking while Minnie plastered his beak and face with wet doggy kisses. I growled at her and put George back up on his feet.

I still wondered why she kept beating up on my little George, until yesterday when I heard him squawking outside the office window. As I peered out I saw the most peculiar thing. George was dancing around in front of Minnie, squawking. When he finally got her attention, he crouched down and rolled onto his back and lay there while she licked his face and beak clean! I finally realised that George didn't have a mother to groom him so he chose the next best thing, Minnie! How does Georgie talk to Minnie?

Can you offer any advice? Contact us at SMARTER than JACK.

3

Smart dogs have fun and outwit others

A dog's sneaky tactics

One day my three-year-old Cavalier King Charles spaniel Ben was chewing a toy on the settee when his brother Charlie decided he wanted it.

Charlie has always been 'top dog' and, whatever he wants, basically he gets. A few dirty looks, and Ben soon gave up the toy.

Ben was sitting a few feet away from Charlie, just looking at him, as though he was wondering how he could get the toy back. It took about 20 minutes and then you could see the penny drop. Ben ran to the back door, barking, so I let him out. Not being the brightest star in the sky, Charlie dropped the toy and ran out after him, whereupon Ben promptly ran back inside to retrieve his toy.

Realising that he'd been 'had', Charlie came inside and took the toy off his brother. I told my husband what had happened and I could see he thought I was making it all up. But then Ben started barking again to get Charlie outside. This time it had taken him only a moment to think how he could fool Charlie.

Mrs Tracey Masters
Billingshurst, West Sussex
England

Ben (right) found a great way to outsmart his brother Charlie (left)

Clever Murphy the fox terrier

Murphy is a black and white foxie with lots of character and personality. The first smart thing Murphy did was running up to Mum at the SPCA (he must have known he was going to a nice home).

The next sign of his intelligence was when he told us Pets Day wasn't for him by chewing through his lead and embarrassing Sam and me when he arrived at the school assembly.

We put him in the ute crate and he managed to squeeze through the bars. The only solution to our problem was to put him in the cab of our ute until it was time for his walk around the ring.

When it was Murphy's turn, Sam went to get him from the ute. As Sam went to open the passenger's door, Murphy sprang up and slammed down the door lock. Sam shot to the other side. Murphy reacted quickly and slammed the driver's door lock down. Since everyone in Weber is so honest, Dad had left the keys in the ute – oh dear! Fortunately the window was down just enough for me to slip my little hand in, unlock the door and save the day.

Murphy loves going out on the farm with Dad. But he is clever enough to know that, if Dad has his good work clothes on, it's no use barking to go with him.

At the end of each day, he again shows us how clever he is. He pretends he's asleep about five minutes before the lights go out. Then out goes the cat – but the sneaky little dog gets the chair for the night.

Andrew McNair
Dannevirke
New Zealand

Andrew and Murphy

Now, how can I get my chair back?

In the 1980s we had two dogs, Pepi and Paddy, both black mongrels. They got on well together and we provided two chairs with no arms for them, side by side.

Pepi had a habit of lying across both chairs. Paddy would walk round the room several times, each time trying to push her off but to no avail. Then he must have remembered that, when the telephone rang, Pepi, being very timid, would leave the room. He would go to the telephone and lift the receiver with his nose, whereupon the bell would tinkle and Pepi would leave the room. Paddy would jump up on his chair with a look on his face that said, *Got it!*

He had another trick up his sleeve. After his usual run around the room he would push his nose into my wife's lap. She would start to make a fuss of him, and Pepi, being very jealous, would jump off the chairs onto her lap. Quick as a flash, Paddy would grab his chair. This happened several times.

Ted Cherrett
Addlestone, Surrey
England

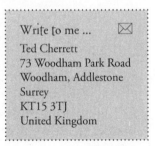

Write to me ... ✉

Ted Cherrett
73 Woodham Park Road
Woodham, Addlestone
Surrey
KT15 3TJ
United Kingdom

She was determined to take her rope

One day I was busy sewing at the table while our two-year-old Labrador/shepherd mix Ebony played with a little piece of chew rope.

Ebony asked to go out, her rope still in her mouth. At our house, one rule is that inside toys are not allowed outside and outside toys cannot be brought in.

I took the rope from her and opened the door but she wouldn't go out. I went back to my sewing, while Ebony continued to go back and forth to the door with her rope and I continued to ignore her, after trying a few times to let her out without the rope.

About 20 minutes later, my boyfriend heard her whining and went to the door to let her out. I told him she had a rope with her and was trying to sneak it outside. He looked all round the porch and didn't see the rope. Thinking Ebony must have to go out and had given up on taking the rope outside, he opened the door. To his surprise, Ebony stuck her nose under the doormat, grabbed her rope and ran out the door.

Serena Saunders
Conception Bay South, Newfoundland
Canada

Timmy's technological breakthrough

My old dog Timmy was named after the canine hero of Enid Blyton's *Famous Five* series. He would not exactly be described as the dog brain of Britain but he wasn't without a certain animal intelligence.

He made a remarkable technological discovery, courtesy of the Tesco supermarket chain.

Here's what happened … I take Timmy to the supermarket after his walk, and instruct him to wait outside for me. It's not our usual shopping place but he knows the drill and sits down obediently, eyes trained on the door, ready to leap up with his usual rapturous welcome as soon as I return. I don't tie him up as I know he will wait.

I go in to find my few items of shopping but get sidetracked at the magazine counter. Decisions of 'Which magazine to buy this week?' sometimes take a while. Aware of being a little longer than expected, I stride briskly to the tills, and when I near the checkout area I notice a small gathering of people by the front door of the supermarket. They are looking at one spot and smiling and laughing, so, never once suspecting that I will live to regret it, I decide to go and see what they're looking at. Such is the nature of human curiosity.

When I see the 'show' they're watching, I am not sure whether to push to the front of the crowd, yelling, 'He's my dog, isn't he wonderful?' or creep away and collect him later. In view of the fact that I am windswept, unmade-up and wearing muddy wellies, I decide to try not to draw attention to myself. Under the circumstances, that's not difficult, because all eyes are focused on the large, hairy black and white performer on centre stage.

Picture this. Peering through his shaggy fringe, Timmy has been watching the doors since I went inside. He has noticed that they open magically as soon as someone walks towards them, and has decided to see whether it works for dogs as well as humans. It does.

Now the resourceful Timmy faces a dilemma. He knows he is not allowed inside (he's in no doubt as to the meaning of 'stay'), but he doesn't recall being told he may not open the door as opposed to going through it. I assume he decides his actions are within the terms of our long-standing agreement.

By this time, he has worked out to the millimetre where his paw has to be to create the miracle, and he is experimenting … Step forward – door opens. Shuffle backwards – door closes. Creep forward on belly – door opens. Keep still – door stays open. Sit on hind legs and wave paws about – door sometimes opens but it seems to depend on whether anyone else is walking through. Bark – nothing happens. Bark some more – still nothing happens.

Timmy, who is always willing to shake a large hairy paw with anyone who pays him any attention at all, is soon performing to his audience. No doubt he thinks they will find his discovery about the doors useful, and it's equally possible he hopes for an edible reward. He is just stepping delicately backwards, tail wagging, to close the doors, when he sees me at the back of the crowd.

He fixes his 'caught in the act' gaze on me, barks once, sits down on the spot (to prove that in spite of outward appearances he is really a good boy), cocks his big tousled head to one side and lifts his paw to say hello. This is typical of him; when all else fails, try 'cute'.

Everyone turns to me. I am painfully aware of uncombed hair and battered old anorak. I'm not ready for the scrutiny of an audience.

'Is that your dog?' someone asks.

I realise that escape is impossible and truth is the only option. 'Er, yes, I think so …' I study him for a minute, hoping for further inspiration which does not come. 'Oh, er, yes … it is.'

'He's sweet,' someone remarks. I smile like a crocodile, for the adjective 'sweet' does not immediately spring to mind.

'He must have got fed up with waiting,' says one.

'She should have tied him up,' agrees her friend. 'I couldn't get my trolley past him,' says another. 'My little girl won't come into the shop,' grumbles a third, 'and he's eaten her chocolate, is he hungry?' I look at the overfed chocolate thief with my 'wait till I get you home' expression but he feigns innocence.

'He's really clever!' says a small boy, and Timmy smirks. I am not mistaken here; I know a smirk when I see one. Someone else strokes his head and he rolls on his back and positively slavers.

 41

The automatic doors provided much amusement for Timmy

'Ah, look. He just wants somebody to tickle his tummy, he wants some attention.' The volunteers press forward. In spite of some hostile looks darting my way, I realise enough is enough and I have to take action. He'll start shoe licking if I don't break up the party.

'Oh, right. Well, thanks. Er, I've just finished here so I'll ...' And as I step through the door with my basket full of unpaid-for goods, the buzzer alerts two security guards.

When it's finally all over and I'm walking away from the supermarket – complete with errant dog, carrier bag and red face – Timmy turns his head to give me a sly, covert look intended to gauge my mood. When I ask him, somewhat sternly, what he thinks he is looking at, he assumes an air of surprise and puts on his nonchalant expression. I can't help smiling, if only at the sheer nerve of the creature.

He sees me smile ... And he changes his shambling walk to an arrogant, self-satisfied swagger. I swear it! I know a swagger when I see one.

Joan Hardy
Stapleford, Nottingham
England

Write to me ...   ✉

email Joan
joan@hardj.freeserve.co.uk

Abi hitched a ride

Abi was my childhood pet. A collie/spaniel cross, she was the brightest dog I've ever met.

As a teenager I was mad on horses and was lucky enough to get my own when I was 13. Abi went with me when I exercised my pony and travelled for miles behind me every day. We would find she'd disappeared, only to discover that she had followed a passing rider, just for the outing. As time went on, everyone who had a horse got to know her and was happy for her to accompany them.

She would tuck herself between the horse and the hedge if we were on main roads or if a car passed by, and if we met an unfriendly dog or had to go through a river – which she hated – she would jump up onto the horse's back behind the rider, and ride along for a while.

Understandably she slowed down as she grew older. This was no problem when I was on the horse, but she couldn't cope when it came to following me on my bike when I cycled down to the horse each day. The main problem was that I had to go down a hill that was one and a half miles long. When she was younger, she kept

 43

with me between bike and hedge, but later she lagged behind. In an attempt to balance herself on the road, she moved out towards the middle if she was left behind, and that wasn't good on a main road.

I tried to cycle very slowly, hands on the brakes so she could keep up. One morning, however, I had the blacksmith coming and had to get to the stables. As I freewheeled down the hill so Abi could keep up, I had an idea. I picked Abi up and sat her on my knees, put her front paws on the handlebars and gently pushed off. As we picked up speed, I thought she would jump off – but no, she loved it. So much better than pounding those tired legs on the concrete.

I'll never forget the looks (and double takes) of the people in the cars that passed us. We freewheeled all the way at great speed, and continued to do the same for a couple of years. I also taught her (or rather she taught me) that she could climb a ladder to help me with the pony's hayloft. I had been trying to devise a plan to hoist her up to the loft, and one day she just followed me gingerly up the ladder.

Emma Thomas
Wallingford, Oxfordshire
England

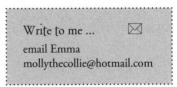

Write to me ...

email Emma
mollythecollie@hotmail.com

A dog plays hide-and-seek

Sheba, my pedigree German shepherd, was extremely intelligent, even for a famously intelligent breed.

Very early on she learned to open every door in the house, by either putting her mouth around a knob or pressing a latch down. For some reason she hated hats, and if I ever put one on for a special occasion she would put her paws on my shoulder to reach it, and pull it off.

Sheba had a great sense of humour

She had a sense of humour, and would play tricks by hiding things from us. She would stand round wagging her tail while we searched frantically. Once, she repeated this every night for several weeks. Around 1 or 2 am she would wake me up, with her bowl in her mouth, asking for a drink. I was obliging enough to get out of bed and refill the bowl. However, she grew tired of this straightforward transaction and began to hide the bowl before she woke me.

I had to go round the house looking for the bowl, which she was clever enough to hide in a different place each time. You might say I could have just ignored her and stayed in bed, but it isn't that easy to ignore a nine-stone-plus German shepherd who is determined to get you out of bed. I'm sure Sheba thoroughly enjoyed watching me

 45

search, while she stood round wagging her tail and 'grinning' in the way some dogs do.

The climax came when I bought her a new bowl as her old one was starting to look somewhat disreputable. I had put the old one aside, intending to dispose of it next day. That night, Sheba came to me as usual. After a long search for her new bowl, I found it stuffed down the toilet.

Needless to say, I returned the old bowl to her. After this incident, the game lost interest for her, and I would once more get a full night's sleep.

Mrs Kathleen Smeaton
Leeds
England

'Buttery toast' was his favourite movie

My one-year-old Westie, Harry, liked nothing better than to eat his favourite food and then hide some for later. Of course it would always be something messy: a jam-covered crumpet, an iced biscuit or a gravy-covered sausage.

To make matters worse, he'd hide it in my clean ironing or in my duvet cover. I'd go round afterwards and collect the soggy item to put in the bin.

One day we gave him half a slice of buttery toast. Half expecting it to end up under the pile of towels on the floor, I was surprised to find there were no leftovers this time. He got praised for eating it all up and not making a mess. Two days later, my family and I were bored so we decided to watch one of our favourite videos. I popped the video in the VCR and was surprised by the tight fit and the funny noise it made as it went in.

We couldn't get the video to play so my dad unscrewed the top of the machine, only to find the video covered in butter. Underneath was the half slice of toast. It seems Harry had got wise to our removal of his buried food and had hidden it somewhere he thought we would never find it.

Emma Reilly
Newcastle upon Tyne
England

An old dog's new tricks

My daughter owns four Labradors. The eldest thinks he is kingpin, for she had him for two years before the others joined him.

One evening she was relaxing on the sofa, one of the other dogs sitting next to her and two others at her feet. The old dog couldn't get near his beloved mistress.

He wandered out into the hall, where he started barking as if someone was at the door. Naturally enough, the other three dogs rushed out to see who it was. The old dog promptly returned to the lounge and climbed up next to his mistress. I thought this was well thought out.

Mrs A Graham
Rustington, West Sussex
England

Bracken had an exceptional talent for finding balls

Bracken the ballboy

Our Bracken was a golden retriever. As a puppy, we taught him how to retrieve things. And the things he liked best were balls. When we threw a ball, he would run after it, collect it and return it to us and we all enjoyed that. But throwing balls makes your arm ache and we stopped doing that – so he started finding his own.

It didn't make any difference *where* it was. Sometimes it was in long grass, or a bush, or a hedge, or even in a wet muddy ditch. Anywhere, it just didn't matter – he would find it and bring it back – even if you didn't know there was one there anyway!

And it didn't make any difference what size or colour it was – it wasn't invisible to him. It could be red or blue or yellow or orange or any colour at all and it could be any size as well, because he brought back golf balls, tennis balls, footballs – any ball would do. If they were made of leather, of rubber, of canvas or even of sponge – it just didn't matter, he'd find one and bring it back – he was a retriever, wasn't he?

The kids in our turning were well pleased. If the ball they were playing with went in the nettles or the brambles, no problem – get Bracken. Football and cricket balls lost by someone – found by Bracken. When Wimbledon was on (which, of course, made tennis popular), Bracken was *the* ballboy. Surplus recoveries of the tennis balls were always donated by Bracken to local kids, local dog owners and local charity shops.

We got used to it over the years, but never really managed to work out *how* he did it. My husband was beginning to believe that the shape of a ball, yes, just the *shape*, must have a distinctive smell all of its own – but Bracken blew that theory by disappearing into the woods one day and coming back with a rugby ball.

So we never discovered the reason for his talent. Exceptional? Certainly. As were his personality, and life for us with him.

Rosemary George
Woking, Surrey
England

Pilot Sam

Driving was Sam's first love. Being a dog, he mastered it by leaning on me. Regardless of my intended direction, Sam would change it. I have seen more telegraph poles one inch from my vehicle's bonnet than most people have.

The day I left him in charge while I dashed across the road for some milk, proved to be his pièce de résistance. Moments later I saw

 49

one brindle boxer sedately cruising downhill in my ancient Velox. 'Stop that dog!' I yelled, waving wildly.

As though it heard me, the car nudged the kerb and stopped gently. Panting, I leaped in, landing on top of Sam who disdainfully dislodged himself. Through the window he perceived an audience – a man who'd initially been watering a bush seemed to be in a state of shock for he was sending a strong jet of H_2O into his gumboot.

Sam rose majestically in the passenger seat to wag his stump of a tail. I swear it was the next best thing to the Queen's wave I've ever seen!

Faie Dana Watson
Burnie, Tasmania
Australia

Write to me ...
Faie Dana Watson
PO Box 801
Burnie
Tasmania 7320
Australia

Not one but three goodnight kisses

I had a rescued Border collie named Jess who managed to get three kisses every night.

She was supposed to spend the nights in her bed in the kitchen. Each evening, as I tidied up the room and prepared to turn out the light, I'd find her already curled up in her bed. The routine was that I'd kneel down and give her a pat and kiss the top of her head, saying, 'Night night, sleep tight.' Then I'd go through to the sitting room and plump up the cushions on the sofa and prepare to switch out those lights.

Without fail, I'd find a Border collie curled up in the armchair by the door, pretending to be asleep. I would say, 'Good heavens, I seem to have a second collie', and once again I would kneel down, pat and kiss the top of her head and say, 'Good night, sleep tight.'

Then upstairs I'd go, first into the bathroom and then along the corridor into my bedroom where I'd turn on the light. Who would I find curled up on the bedside rug but a third collie! Once the same ritual had been played out, I would undress and get into bed, switching off the light. The only sound in the dark bedroom was my dear collie thumping her tail on the rug, obviously pleased with her play-acting. Once again she had managed to get three goodnight kisses instead of one, and I just *knew* she was smiling.

Pat Sequeira
Reigate, Surrey
England

Jess found a way to get three goodnight kisses

Hurry up and put your shoes on!

Sam, my English springer spaniel, was fixated on shoes.

Returning family members were always greeted with the gift of a shoe. Sam would hide them, so he'd always have a present handy. Many appointments were missed and folks made late because of a missing shoe.

If you ignored his hints about going for a walk, he would rummage in the shoe cupboard, pick out a pair of walkers and fling them at your feet.

Another passion was tea. He adored it and always begged for some in his bowl. A couple of times he sneaked into an afternoon tea party, sidled up to an unattended china teacup and carried it away by the handle, hiding behind the sofa to enjoy his ill-gotten gains.

In spite of his wicked sense of fun, he was loving, loyal and brave.

Sue Miller
London, Ontario
Canada

4

Smart dogs look out for us

Sixth sense

After days of torrential rains and high winds, the sun finally appeared. Taj, my Border collie, looked hopeful, then excited when he realised we were going out.

Dodging puddles became a game as we set out along the gravel path. Our walk progressed smoothly until, for no apparent reason, Taj stopped in the middle of the path and flatly refused to move. No matter what I said or did, he wouldn't budge.

Suddenly there was a loud creaking sound followed by a thunderous crash. Startled, I looked up. A large tree branch had fallen down onto the path ahead of us. If Taj hadn't stopped me from moving I would have been exactly underneath it.

Badly shaken, I looked down at my clever dog, gave him the biggest cuddle of his life and wondered how he knew what was going to happen.

As for Taj, he straightened up, shook his thick fur coat and, now that I was out of danger, prepared to continue his walk.

Rosalina McCarthy
Nelson
New Zealand

Write to me ... ✉
email Rosalina at:
rosalina@xtra.co.nz

🐕 53

Taj and Rosalina

The dog's sense of smell was better than mine

My dog Jerimiah is a cockapoo (poodle/cocker spaniel cross) and he is the love of my life.

I am an artist and often bring my dogs to my work teaching art with seniors and children. We spend a lot of time together as much of my work is home-based.

I was heating up potatoes in a stainless steel pot and unwisely had the burner on high. My nose was stuffed up with a cold and I didn't smell the pot beginning to burn.

I started working on my computer in another room. Jerimiah came to sit beside me, staring at me and making funny breathing noises to get my attention. I ran to the kitchen as the house filled with smoke. I put the pot outdoors, opened all the doors and put the fan on to clear the house.

Jerimiah was indeed speaking to me.

Norene Procter
Calgary, Alberta
Canada

Merlot protected my family from 'stranger danger'

When my first grandchild was a baby, my daughter Helen asked if she could take the dog out with them for a walk. I had an Irish setter/greyhound cross named Merlot, who was energetic and extremely loyal.

They went to the riverbank, where Merlot went into the bush to chase rabbits as usual. There was no one else around when Helen, walking with Byron in the pushchair, noticed a man approaching. He wore a long black coat, looked unkempt and stared at her intently. She began to feel uncomfortable.

 55

Helen was wondering where Merlot was, when he suddenly burst out of the bushes, looked from the man to Helen and then walked towards the man. He kept ahead of Helen and then, as the stranger came abreast, positioned himself between them, and when they passed he dropped back, keeping between the two. Once the man was apparently judged to be a safe distance away, he went off to chase rabbits again.

When Helen told me about this incident, she said she did not call Merlot or speak to him once he appeared, but kept walking. She and I believe that Merlot showed protective behaviour towards Helen and little Byron.

Heather Goffin
Palmerston North
New Zealand

Write to me ... ✉
email Heather at:
merloette@paradise.net.nz

Merlot protected Helen and Byron

Dog stayed with our daughter

Our dog came to us from the empty lands of the Desert Road, with bleeding paws – skin and bone. He thrived with us, but we never did agree on a name so he became Dog.

He was mixed breed, probably with some Labrador and Great Dane as he was big and easy-going. We guessed he'd come from a farm as he had no idea of the safety of the pedestrian area versus the road.

One day our toddler went missing. We were living in a rented house, having moved to a new town, and she found a way out of the garden. My husband found her, out on the road but not alone. Dog was with her, walking in a tight curve around her, staying with her as if he knew this was not a place she should be. We loved him even more for it.

Barbara Hock
Rotorua
New Zealand

The farm dogs kept me safe

My favourite place when I was young was my aunt and uncle's dairy farm.

My mother and I used to go there for the school holidays. My aunt, now 95 and in a nursing home, tells many stories of my adventures on the farm. Once, I remember wandering off to the 'danger paddock' while Mum and my aunt collected eggs from the hen house. My best friends were Goofy and Tippy, the cattle dogs. They would follow me everywhere and get me out of some sticky situations!

My aunt would say, 'Don't go into the end paddock 'cause the bull might hurt you.' Well, we all know what 'Don't' means to a child. Guess where I was? Yep, in with the bull.

My mother and aunt were trying to find me, when they looked to where the dogs were barking. Goofy had hold of my jumper and was pulling me away from the bull and towards the gate, while Tippy was barking to keep the bull in check and to alert my mother and aunt.

Goofy and Tippy saved the day – and me – again.

Jeanine Styler
West Brunswick, Victoria
Australia

Time to wake up?

Pujji, an English Staffordshire bull terrier, was less than a year old when we moved into our new home. So was the house, with its attendant minor problems. After Pujji had been house-trained she was finally allowed to sleep indoors, but was restricted to a couch downstairs.

However, during the next few months she came to the top of the stairs several times. She stopped at the low barrier there, and cried until I woke up.

The first time she woke me, I could hear the sound of a smoke detector indicating that the backup battery was low on power. I went down and quietened the noise, appreciating her intelligence.

The second time, I couldn't hear anything and wondered if she needed to go outside to relieve herself. When I felt the blast of cold air, I realised the wind had blown open the front door, which I obviously hadn't shut properly.

On the third occasion, I just happened to be awake and watching TV in bed when the power blacked out for a second. The TV turned off and on, and I could see the light of one of the exterior sensor lights had illuminated as well. But within a moment Pujji was at the top of the stairs and gave a little cry. I smiled to myself, and thought that I'd just walk her back to her couch as a way of rewarding her for her vigilance.

I was surprised to see the whole outside of the house was illuminated, since all the sensor lights had tripped themselves on simultaneously. She'd seen one or two lights come on individually, but never several lights at once. She figured this must be a time to wake me up.

She's come to the stairs a number of times since, and has woken me up not by crying, but just by knocking at the barrier. That's her call for me to let her outside for a moment. By day, this translates into a sharp bark, if no one's looking in her direction.

Casey Herman
Noble Park, Victoria
Australia

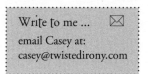

Write to me ...
email Casey at:
casey@twistedirony.com

Tripper the smoke detector

It was back in 1981 and my wife was away from home, visiting her parents. I was looking after the house, my two sons and our five-year-old dog Tripper.

One evening I returned from a full day at work, fed Tripper his evening meal and saw the boys off on a visit to their friends. I decided to make pasta for dinner so put a pot of water to boil on the electric stove. Then I retired to the den to watch TV.

 59

I fell asleep but was woken by Tripper, who was standing right between my knees and barking at me. I saw smoke in the next room and remembered about the pot of water. I rushed to the kitchen, where I saw flames as high as the stove hood. I put the pot in the sink, opened the door and got myself and Tripper outside.

Tripper could have got out through the doggy door in the kitchen but he'd come to awaken me, and for that I was grateful. The irony was that there was no smoke alarm in the house at the time. We lost no time installing two detectors at potential danger areas.

Tripper was with us for 21 good years.

Edwin and Louise Levigne
Coquitlam, British Columbia
Canada

Oh, great, you have to go out …

My brother acquired Bobbie, a fawn pug, as a companion for our mother during the daytime.

Some years later, my brother did the laundry on Saturday night and went to bed, forgetting to turn off the water valves to the washing machine. As luck would have it, he was also cleaning up the recreation room and had moved his stereo, microwave and treadmill into the area where the washing machine was.

About 1 am, Bobbie jumped on my brother's bed and pressed his nose into his face (people who have pugs will relate to this tactic). My brother woke up and thought, 'Oh, great, you have to go out.' But, as he went to open the outside door, Bobbie became agitated and instead went down the stairs into the basement. My brother followed him and heard a loud hissing sound.

The hose connecting the water to the washing machine had sprung a leak and water was spraying everywhere, including all over his stereo and microwave. My brother turned off the water and Bobbie turned, ran upstairs and went back to bed. The damage done was minimal, which meant the leak had only started a few minutes before. If it had gone undetected, it would have continued for at least seven hours – which would have meant extensive damage, not only to all the equipment but also to the rest of the basement area.

Our mother was proud of her little pug and bragged about his intelligence to anyone who would listen.

Pat
Calgary, Alberta
Canada

Bobbie's timely warning saved the day

 61

She was making the most appalling noise

My tiny Yorkshire terrier was always special to me, but once she revealed a side to her character that I knew nothing about.

I'd had an unfortunate experience in a local hospital through mismanagement, neglect and dirtiness. As soon as I was able, I complained by letter, saw the seniors involved and was promised that the situation would immediately be rectified. I checked afterwards and, indeed, it had been done. All I wanted was to make sure others didn't have to suffer as I had done.

However, I began to get calls from a very pushy man who wanted me to let him 'take up my case' against the NHS (National Health Service). Each time, I told him I did not want this and put the phone down. It was strange but he always rang while my husband was at church. Now, I believe in the NHS – with all its faults – and did not want to try to get money from them which could be better spent on the patients.

On the last morning he rang he seemed to be getting very annoyed, and shortly after I put the phone down yet again, there was a knock at the front door. When I opened it I was almost pushed over by a large gentleman. He pushed past me and sat himself down at my kitchen table where I was preparing vegetables for our midday meal. He proceeded to harangue me again on the same subject.

He shouted and waved his arms about, and although I'm not easily frightened I started to feel decidedly uneasy. Suddenly Erna, my little dog, dashed in from the garden, making the most appalling noise – barking, snarling and growling. I was amazed, as normally she was amiable with people. She was trying desperately to get to this man, so I grabbed her.

He stammered, 'Does she bite?' and my brain started to work. I replied, 'Oh yes, *frequently*.' He got up rapidly, dashed for the door, let himself out and flung himself into a large dark green car. I have had no more trouble from him.

I carried Erna back to the kitchen, rolled her on the floor and rubbed her tummy (which she always loved) and said, 'Erna, I didn't know you could snarl, I didn't know you could growl.' She went all wiggly waggly and gave one last enormous *snarl*, laughing all over her tiny face.

She was normally the friendliest, quietest, tamest little friend you could envisage. She was given to me by my eldest daughter as a 'thank you' for looking after my grandsons for four months. The only thing she used to bite was her food!

She died at the grand old age of 16, and she lives on in my heart.

Ann Godden
Thorpe Green, Surrey
England

Inca knew when my distress was genuine

I adopted Inca via Dalmatian Rescue. She was scared of all men, especially those with hats and beards, and wary of anything or anyone who moved behind or above her. Her head was scarred from being hit and she was frequently lame, due to poor diet and lack of care at her previous home. She was frightened of the lead and didn't know how to play with toys.

A few months after I took her, I was diagnosed with a severe back problem. One evening, as I went to get up from lying on the floor, my back 'locked' and I was unable to move an inch. I froze, scared to move, as every attempt resulted in excruciating pain.

Without any prompting or calling, Inca leaped out of her bed and rushed over to me. She licked my face as if she were trying to

 63

Inca (right) with friend Lima

reassure me, lay down and crawled on her belly underneath me. Slowly she began to raise herself until her back was touching my stomach. She flexed her muscles and began to stand up, lifting me as she did so. Once she had fully stood up, she remained perfectly still, enabling me to support myself against her and some furniture and finally get to my feet. As soon as she saw me standing, she turned and went back to her bed.

Some time later, when I was feeling better, I thought I would put Inca to the test. I knelt down on my hands and knees and waited, pretending to be 'stuck'. But this time Inca just sat and stared. She made no attempt to come to me. It was obvious that no one could fool her.

Several weeks later, my back 'locked' again and, as before, Inca sprang into action. She rushed over to me, crawled under me and slowly raised me up. This has now happened numerous times. On the few occasions I've 'faked' it, she has totally ignored me.

Inca has never been trained to do this. It's truly amazing that she can work out for herself when there's a genuine need for help. She is the most loyal and affectionate friend I've had the pleasure of owning. I rescued Inca once – but she has come to my rescue dozens of times.

W Bennett
Worcestershire
England

A non-smoking campaigner

My husband had a mongrel dog, a stray adopted by his family. They were unable to trace his previous owner so kept him, and called him Toby.

Perhaps a clue to his past was the fact that he got agitated if anyone smoked when he was around.

As soon as they threw a cigarette butt down on the ground, Toby would jump on it and stamp on it, with stiff front paws held together, until the cigarette end was totally obliterated. At the same time, he would make little whimpering noises. They felt that something to do with fire had perhaps caused him to get lost, since he showed such agitation at the sight of fire. He seemed to recognise that a cigarette meant fire, and had taught himself to put the fire out.

Patricia Williams
Weybridge, Surrey
England

Write to me ...   ✉
email Patricia at:
pviwilliams2@tiscali.co.uk

Fillipa and Rupert

Fillipa knew something was wrong

Our Cavalier King Charles spaniel Fillipa came to live with us at seven months when it became apparent that her future wasn't in the show ring. She became companion and guardian to our deaf Cavalier Rupert, who sadly suffers from syringomyelia.

She and Rupert were staying overnight with our friend Heather and her three children. That night Fillipa would not settle so Heather took them both out for a walk.

Fillipa became agitated and, when they turned round to go home, she pulled badly – not her normal behaviour at all. They ended up running most of the way back.

Home again, Rupert settled in 13-year-old Jennifer's room. Fillipa went upstairs with Heather but still wouldn't settle. Heather became quite firm but she just kept barking. This was most unusual as she was sensitive and hated being told off. Heather decided to see if Fillipa had woken the children with her barking. But when she opened the door to nine-year-old Samantha's room, it was full of smoke. Samantha was asleep, so Heather woke her and opened all the windows.

Once everything was sorted out, Fillipa settled straight away. No one else had smelt the smoke as Heather had been baking and the whole house smelt of bread. The fire had arisen from a piece of damp kitchen roll which Samantha had put on top of the bulb in her bedside lamp. She'd fallen asleep with the lamp still on.

Mrs Nicki Hughes
Brora, Sutherland
Scotland

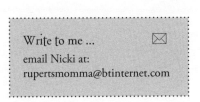

Write to me ...

email Nicki at:
rupertsmomma@btinternet.com

Henry raised the alarm

My son got a Labrador/bull terrier cross from the Dogs' Home in Gütersloe after his beloved German shepherd died.

A few months after we got Henry, I was alone in the house, writing letters. My son's house was quite large and my room was at the far end. Henry dashed into my room, making guttural sounds, then dashed out again. He kept doing this until I said, 'Now what have you done, Henry? Let's go and see.' He ran into the kitchen and, when I went in, it was to find the electrical switches on the washing machine were on fire! I dread to think what might have happened if Henry hadn't raised the alarm.

Needless to say, Henry got a lot of titbits from Grandma after that. I will always remember the day he saved me.

Barbara Welby
Emsworth, Hampshire
England

Henry alerted his 'grandma' to danger

5

Smart dogs take control

Sheba took her duties seriously

Sheba was one of four puppies left at the gate of my sister's boarding kennels. She was the runt of the litter and we decided to keep her. She grew up with my children and they couldn't go anywhere without her following.

My parents had a bach at Tinopai and the kids loved to go swimming whenever they could. As they splashed around with their armbands and kickboards, Sheba would be paddling around and looking after her brood. But once she'd had enough, everyone had to get out of the water.

First she'd take one kickboard to shore, using her mouth. She'd swim out for the next, much to the kids' disgust as by then they knew what was in store. She would swim out, grab hold of an armband and, as it deflated, proceed to tow the disgruntled child ashore. With the child safely on the beach, she would head out to retrieve the other child, who by this time was trying desperately to get ashore before she too had only one armband.

Another time, the kids were playing at the neighbours' house. I called them to come home for their bath and dinner. Just as they were getting into the bath we heard a terrible noise coming from the driveway. We looked out to see Sheba with the handle of a plastic ride-on motorbike in her mouth, pulling the bike home. Once in the gate she dropped it and turned smartly back up the road to get the other bike.

The kids are adults now. They tell me that Sheba should have been named 'Mum'.

Odele Fenton
Huntly
New Zealand

Sheba made sure she took good care of her 'brood'

I'll make them feed me

Okey, our Jack Russell terrier, knows exactly when it's time to eat. Like her peers, this is mostly all the time, but there are set hours when she feels the need to remind us who is in charge of her catering needs.

She barks out the message, jumps on laps, scatters books and newspapers, destroys games of patience or simply guides us to her bowl. But one evening she came up with a new dodge.

We were engrossed in a television programme. After several reminders, which we ignored, she jumped off an unresponsive lap and made for the TV. She pawed the video cabinet door open and started scratching at the switches in an apparent attempt to turn the video off.

She couldn't find the right switch, but her ploy succeeded. Who could carry on watching the programme after that?

Sheelagh Marwood
Weston-super-Mare, North Somerset
England

Staying overnight was forbidden

I am disabled and operate a nightly ministry among the homeless and street folk in the suburbs near my home. One night I saw an animal hiding in one of the squats, and after six long weeks of my leaving food, it finally allowed me to get close.

It was a young dog, a schipperke as I discovered later. I thought at first that her tail had been docked but it's not uncommon for this breed to have no tail. After a couple more weeks she was confident enough to allow me to take her to a vet to be checked over. She was

 71

Jeze became a bouncer

in reasonable health, although badly malnourished and neglected, and we made a mutual decision to adopt each other. I called her Jeze.

We became devoted to each other and Jeze quickly learned how to walk with me when I was using my frame. She preferred me to use my scooter, where she'd perch on my lap. She found that by depressing a certain lever she could make the scooter move. If I'd stopped to chat to people, I had to remember to disengage the key so she could not decide that it was time to go.

Shortly after she came to live with me, my son came to visit. As it was getting late, he decided to stay overnight. Jeze accepted his presence until it became evident that he was setting up a bed for himself on the couch.

Jeze paced between my bedroom and the living room. Then she started whimpering and sitting by the back door. Thinking she wanted to go out, my son obligingly opened the door for her, only to have Jeze grab the leg of his jeans and start pulling him outside.

Obviously, visiting was one thing but overnight stays were definitely not permitted as far as she was concerned. I had to intervene to stop her efforts to evict my son.

They are good friends now, but my son has never forgotten how this small dog became a bouncer.

Margaret Richardson
Blackburn South, Victoria
Australia

A referee of a different kind

Randy, our eight-year-old Border collie, loves to work with horses.

She is an avid observer at horse shows and always knows in advance when something is about to go wrong on the showjumping course. Seconds before it happens, when everybody is still thinking that the current contestant is doing great, she starts whimpering and wants to get onto the course. Not long afterwards, the horse will start behaving petulantly or stop in front of the next obstacle. We have to keep her on the leash to prevent her from pushing rider and horse back on the right course, and it is very hard to keep her quiet!

 73

I used to participate in horse shows myself and Randy was my personal mascot. One day she took her 'job' very seriously. I was on a jumping course with a five-year-old gelding called Artus. The jumping itself was not normally a problem, but sometimes Artus wanted to leave the course early and I had to force him back. This time we had got over four obstacles already and we were approaching the exit. Looking forward to carrots and hay at the trailer, he started getting cheeky and pressed towards the exit. I was concentrating so hard on keeping him on the course that I did not realise Randy was barking loudly and coming to help. She nipped Artus's hind legs and succeeded in making him submissive again.

Of course, we did not win a prize but we crossed the finishing line, and from that day on Randy only had to bark once when Artus tried again to disobey his rider and he'd start behaving again.

Leonie Buhl
Lichtenau
Germany

Tandy went to see for herself

My husband and I, along with two friends and our golden Labrador Tandy, went on holiday to Looe in Cornwall in 1989. Tandy would have been ten years old.

One late afternoon we walked along the sea wall and looked out to sea. We could see a large rectangular object bobbing up and down on the horizon, a long way out. Along with a few other people who had gathered and were also intrigued as to what it might be, we stood for a while, discussing it.

Tandy sat quietly with us and then, without anyone saying anything, she leaped from the sea wall, bounded across the beach

Tandy decided to see what all the fuss was about

and into the sea, and began to swim towards the object. The sea was very choppy and soon she was so far out we could no longer see her. We called frantically for her to come back, worrying that she would be drowned.

As we stood waiting for what seemed like an age, we could see the mystery object gradually moving closer to shore. As it, and her, slowly emerged from the deep, she shook herself and dropped the article at our feet, barking excitedly. It was an old fisherman's gaiter!

I'm sure Tandy enjoyed the spontaneous applause and pats on the back she got from the other onlookers. She seemed none the worse for her expedition.

 75

I don't know what made her do it, as no one told her to. The sea was far too rough. In her own way, perhaps she understood what we were saying and decided to sort out the problem. She was a smart dog, always eager to please. She has gone now but I think of her often. I'm sure animals understand a lot more than we give them credit for.

Mrs J Wright
Leicester, Leicestershire
England

Bella decided who her family would be

Winnie, our eight-year-old kelpie/Lab cross, was known as 'the Queen', due to the love and devotion showered on her by the whole family. Taking walks often meant first driving to an industrial area to avoid other dogs. Winnie wasn't keen on unfamiliar dogs. She did have canine friends, though, and Coach was her favourite.

An awesome animal, Coach was well known to the council dog rangers as king of the district. He could regularly be seen roaming around, surveying his kingdom. Of indeterminable parentage, his genes were obviously the result of mixing powerful breeds.

Coach waited faithfully on our front lawn every day for Winnie to return from her walk, greeting her warmly with lots of kisses and much display. One morning as we approached the house I could see Coach in our yard, lying on his side, with a black puppy curled up and snuggled against his massive chest.

As we got out of the car, the puppy came running over like a long-lost friend. I bent down and asked her name. 'It should be Bella because you're so beautiful,' I said, and she jumped up and licked my face. So Bella she was from that moment.

Wearing no collar or ID, there was no immediate way to investigate where she had come from. So for the next few days we were graced with her lovely presence while I rang local vets and pounds.

On about day three, a man and his two children spotted my son Sean walking Bella and approached him, saying that she was their dog. Sean dutifully handed her over.

A few days later Sean came home very upset, saying that he went to check how the puppy was doing and witnessed the children being cruel to Bella and teasing her.

Unsure if the situation was serious enough to report, I worried all day. That night I snuck over to see for myself. Sadly Sean was not exaggerating, and the children were taking their lead from their parents. I resolved to call the RSPCA in the morning.

Before I had the chance to make that call, my ex-husband arrived with Bella in tow, saying she'd come out of nowhere and followed him. She had met him only very briefly on that first day.

It was with a very heavy heart that we decided to deliver her to the local vet, with a detailed report on the treatment she was subjected to by her owners. Handing Bella over to the nurse that day was agonising, and the expression on her face mirrored my own. I'll never forget that look.

After two miserable days spent feeling sick over the fate of this darling little girl, I was sitting in a room with the French doors fully opened to let the sun in. Anyone wanting to get to the front door would need to walk past these doors, making it virtually impossible for me to be taken by surprise.

Nevertheless I was surprised to hear a knock, and jumped up out of the chair immediately, taking only seconds to open the door. There she was, sitting like a good girl, wagging the tip of her tail.

While I looked round for whoever had knocked, Bella raced through the house at breakneck speed. Finally she settled next to

 77

Winnie on the lounge, with a very satisfied air about her. There was no trace of the knocker.

I'm sure she knew that, if she persisted long enough, I would eventually realise she belonged with us. And on that day I did, deciding that her owners would have to come and face me in order to get her back – praying fervently that they would not.

It's been four years now and the abusive owners have moved. Although they saw us together many times before they left, thankfully they never lifted a finger to reclaim her.

Tragically for us, Winnie became fatally ill about eight months after Bella arrived. Coming back from the vet's that last time without Winnie, I couldn't look at Bella, feeling great guilt about a promise I'd made Winnie. Every day I'd say, 'I love you so much, Win, you're the best girl for me and I'd never swap you for another.'

Irrational as it was, in my grief I felt that I'd swapped Winnie for Bella. But by the second day I noticed Bella wasn't eating and would not come away from Winnie's bed. The poor little darling was grieving as much as the rest of the family. From that moment on we became a great support for each other.

Bella has proved her loyalty many times over in the past four years, and her superior intelligence is unquestioned by all who know her.

Trish Haywood
Daceyville, Sydney
Australia

6

Smart dogs to the rescue

Lindy knew he needed help

It was a snowy afternoon – practically a blizzard – when my husband and our Border collie Lindy set off on foot to feed two horses we were looking after.

While they were with the horses my husband suffered a brain haemorrhage, which affected his balance. He managed to get about a hundred yards from home, when he slipped down in the snow and was unable to get up. A woman passed by on her way from work and he called to her for help, but by now it was dark and lonely and when she heard a man's voice she hurried on to catch her bus.

However, Lindy knew my husband needed help. She kept running up to the road and back, barking, until the woman realised that something must be wrong. She went to investigate, phoned for an ambulance, got additional help, and I was located and informed.

It was touch and go for my husband, but against the odds he pulled through and eventually made a good recovery. If Lindy hadn't gone for help, the ending could have been very different. She was also my constant companion for the four months he was in hospital.

Mrs Sheila Evans
Chesham, Buckinghamshire
England

Tia brought Amanda back from a dangerous out-of-body experience

Sherry saved my life

I was at the beach one day in late summer. I was only ten and not a good swimmer, and the waves were huge.

Realising that I could no longer touch the seabed, I panicked and went under. My family didn't notice anything, but my dog Sherry must have seen me. She swam out to where I was (by this time I was very far out), turned around so that I could hold her tail and pulled me back to the shore.

She died last year but I will never forget what she did.

K Burridge
Dorset
England

You're out of danger now

Tia, my Rottweiler, regularly gave demonstrations that showed what an extraordinarily talented dog she was. She even had acting appearances on TV and was a real-life 'Lassie'. But by far the smartest thing she ever did, just three months before I had to have her euthanised, was to save my life.

I was away on a house-sitting job in May 2004, and in the early hours of the morning I was asleep in bed, Tia sleeping by the side of my bed.

Suddenly I became aware that I was gasping for air, completely unable to breathe in or out, open my eyes or move my body. My lungs felt as though they were about to burst. All I could do was turn my head from side to side, trying to free the obstruction blocking my airway, but to no avail.

I began to fall away from my body, dropping out of it through my upper back. I was fearful and knew I was out of control. It was

 81

an indescribable sensation; I was separating from my body. Feeling panicked about falling into the vast emptiness below me, I said, 'I don't want to be doing this, I'm going to fall', but nothing and no one took any notice. I continued to come away from my body, and parted from it completely. I hadn't fallen and plummeted into nothingness after all, but instead, very gently and slowly, I was floating down, away from my body.

I was becoming completely at ease; the further I drifted away, the less I became aware of gasping for air. As I floated down, I wondered where I was going to end up, but I didn't care. I felt peaceful and totally relaxed as I slowly continued to drift further and further away.

High up above me and to my right, I could just hear Tia barking. It was so very far, far away in the distance, and a tone of bark I'd never heard before. A very soft and gentle bark.

Suddenly my whole body's response was, 'I've got to get to Tia.' I stopped falling instantly, and started to journey back up, still out of control and a passenger but at twice the speed at which I had been floating down. All the time I was rising, I had an urgent need to get to Tia. As I approached the re-entering of my body, I expected that same indescribable though not unpleasant sensation to happen again. And it did. Completely inside myself once more, I quickly sat up in bed, pushing the duvet away from my face. It had been suffocating me. I reached my hand down to make contact with Tia, to rest it on her side gently, as I always did when I wanted to let her know that everything was okay.

Her subsequent behaviour was unusual. With her ears erect and her eyes like saucers, she stared very intensely at me, straight into my eyes. She held this penetrating stare, looking hard and deep into me. I could feel she was telling me, *You're out of danger now*. She held this intense stare a few moments longer, then lay flat out on her side and went back to sleep as though nothing had happened, knowing I was now out of danger.

Apart from having a head which felt like a squashed tomato for about an hour afterwards because of the lack of oxygen, the tearful shock of it all didn't hit home until the next morning. Then I realised what she had done for me.

Tia had given me the ultimate gift a dog can give its owner. She had saved my life. It's the most immensely precious, weird and tender feeling, knowing you owe your life to your dog, a completely different species. I know that had Tia not been with me to call me back from the out-of-body experience I was having, I wouldn't be here today to tell you this story. Instead, I would have suffocated in my sleep.

Amanda Hawes
Henley-on-Thames, Oxfordshire
England

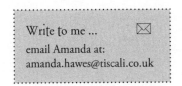

Write to me ...
email Amanda at:
amanda.hawes@tiscali.co.uk

Randy and the rabbit

Our Border collie Randy is not a trained herding dog, and we never had any sheep. But she has always acted the part like a natural.

She circuits in the opposite direction when we lunge horses, and looks after them when they are out at feed. That has caused a few 'occupational accidents' because horses are more stubborn than cattle or sheep.

She tried to keep our rabbit Gypsy, who liked to run wild several hours a day, in order. Sometimes we've had to order Randy back, as Gypsy was too old to really accustom herself to the dog and would duck anxiously when nosy Randy came too close.

 83

One day they were both in the garden when Randy barked suddenly. We quickly realised that something was going on and went outside, where we saw Randy standing protectively over Gypsy. Our neighbour's new dog was trying to catch the rabbit. Randy obviously wanted to make sure that Gypsy was all right and had called us for help.

I had already lost Gypsy's forerunner Mimi through a dog attack and it had taken a long time before I decided to get another one. So Randy was a lifesaver.

Leonie Buhl
Lichtenau
Germany

Bracken's story - from humble beginnings

We adopted our Border collie Bracken when she was eight weeks old. She had been the subject of a prosecution and was taken in by Border Collie Rescue in Anglesey.

When she was 18 months old she began two years' training with the Search and Rescue Dog Association. My husband is a Mountain Rescue volunteer, and Bracken became one of the best dogs in the association. In January 2000 she obtained the title Novice Search Dog, and the following month she and Pete were called out to look for a family who'd become lost in fog at night on Pendle Hill, Lancashire.

They searched for 45 minutes, when Bracken indicated to Pete that she'd found something. Sure enough, the father and three children and their dog were sheltering behind a rock. Their two-year-old was becoming hypothermic, and it doesn't bear thinking about what might have happened had the family been out all night.

Two weeks later, Bracken found a young woman alive and well after she had been missing for three days. Not all her finds have had such happy endings, as in 2004 she uncovered a murder victim, and was also involved in a search on Morecambe Bay for missing cocklers. In August 2004 she was awarded the Man's Best Friend award by *Dogs Today* at the Windsor Wag and Bone Show.

I observe the way Bracken and Pete look at each other, an wonder if there is another partnership anywhere which is as close. They seem to understand each other without any words or barks being exchanged. Bracken goes along with our younger Border collie Fly to compete in fly ball and, while she enjoys her new hobby, she enjoys her 'day job' even more.

Irene Shaw
Poulton-Le-Fylde, Lancashire
England

Write to me ...

email Pete and Irene Shaw at:
dog1pete@hotmail.com

Bracken is an award-winning search and rescue dog

85

Come quick, my friend needs help

When Amber, my rescued Border collie cross, was nine months old I took her to stay with a friend. She had an elderly rough-coated collie bitch who was very stiff in her back legs.

Having settled both dogs downstairs for the night, we retired to our respective bedrooms. About half past two I was woken by a gentle but persistent whining at my door.

Outside, Amber was running anxiously to the top of the stairs and back to my room. My friend and I crept nervously downstairs, where we found Amber crouching under the hall table. And there was the older dog, stuck fast in the corner where she had slid on the tiles. Her back legs were folded uncomfortably beneath her and she was too stiff to extricate herself.

We helped her out, checked that all was well and, with the help of a tasty biscuit, put her back to bed. Amber curled up at her side and went to sleep. But for her intervention, the old dog would have spent an uncomfortable night trapped under the table.

Val Castle
West Ewell, Surrey
England

She sought help for her mate

Some years ago I was awakened by the sounds of barking and whimpering. They seemed to come from one of the houses up the road from ours, and I thought the owner would surely get up and attend to it, for the noise must have woken others besides me.

The barking persisted to such a degree that eventually I got up to open a window and determine what it was all about. It seemed to come from a patch of unused woodland on the other side of the road, some 300 yards away. I realised that the dog must have no connection with any of the other houses, so I dressed and went outside to see if I could do anything to put a stop to what must be a dog in distress.

As I approached, the barking stopped but the whimpering, which was coming from the centre of this small woodland copse, continued. It was really too dark for me to do anything to help, so I hung about for a bit, trying to appease the animal. As this seemed to have the desired effect and the dog seemed not to be in pain, I decided to go home and leave the situation until morning. The howling continued on and off for the rest of the night, and I must confess I wondered if the dog had been caught in a trap or snare.

I returned to the scene at daybreak. When I went into the copse I came across a small, very agitated black and white, smooth-coated mongrel bitch. It was wagging its tail but at the same time whimpering its head off. In the centre of the copse was an early seventeenth century ice house designed to supply ice for the mansion close by and for the people of the village. The little dog was causing quite a hullabaloo at the entrance to the ice house.

I drew closer to see why, only to hear another dog whimpering from the bottom of the ice house. It had obviously fallen in, and was apparently mate to the bitch causing all the commotion. She'd been trying to attract someone's attention so they could rescue her friend.

I left the pair of them and went to phone the RSPCA. A black and tan dog was eventually taken out of the ice house. When they were reunited, the joy they both showed at being together again was indeed rewarding. It later transpired that the two dogs belonged to some gypsies working on roads in the area, and that they had been on the loose and had gone off on a day's hunting together.

 87

What was so pleasing was the affection the two animals had for each other, especially the bitch's affection for her mate and the effort she made to get help to save his life.

G Philip Rimington
Wrexham, Clwyd
Wales

A 'rescue' dog rescues her master

A lifetime ago, we left England behind and went to live on a smallholding in the remote Shetland Islands, about as far as it's possible to get from anywhere else without actually leaving the country and yet still be a world apart.

It was our home for the next 16 years, along with a menagerie of chickens, lambs, goats, pigs, rabbits, four cats and the eight whippets who made the journey with us. Of the dogs, five were three generations of the same family and one was a star in his own right, having had a brief role in a popular BBC comedy. The other two – Penny and her son Fred – were 'rescue' dogs. For a long time Fred remained shy and distant, yet from our first meeting Penny, so full of trust and love, was joyous at their release. That they had survived so much and were still together was, to me, nothing short of a miracle.

For those born there, and for those who can stay, Shetland is a strange land. As befits this far northern outpost of ancient Viking settlers, it is a place of both rugged beauty and wild extremes. Summer – with daylight 24 hours long, rolling heather hills and steel blue seas – contrasts starkly with long dark winter nights, where flickering northern lights are often one's only company. And then there's the wind … screaming gales that last for weeks on end, turn the grass black with salt spray and occasionally leave tractors upended in the fields or tankers strewn on rocks. I once slept soundly through a 148 miles per hour hurricane, only to find the following morning that the house next door had been completely demolished. In Shetland the wind has a mind of its own, and all too often a wild sense of humour to match.

It was during one such winter that Penny saved the day. The gale had been howling for four days solid, simply the latest in a succession that swept the North Sea, a steady Force Nine that shook all the windows and, when it came, drove rain horizontally. I was out doing the rounds, wrapped in oilskins and zipped up against the wind, to collect eggs and feed the animals. As always, it was a battle simply to get around the corner of the house and out to each building.

In these conditions, opening doors – whether car or house – is always the trickiest part. The first year we arrived, the wind took the door off the Land Rover, simply because I wasn't quick enough. Depending on the direction, getting it shut could become the problem, and with a door or window wide open, any roof will start to creak ominously.

On this occasion, I managed to unbolt the door and squeeze in through the gap before fastening it on the inside. For the next 20 minutes or so, thankful for shelter, I tended to the animals and spent some time rearranging bales of hay and bags of feed in the storeroom, while around me the whole building flexed and strained. The wind was savaging everything outside and tearing around like a mad thing.

Finally, having made sure everything was secure, I prepared to do battle with the elements once more. I took a firm hold of the door and lifted the catch, ready to slip out between gusts. But the door

 89

wouldn't open. The wind, forever playing tricks, had spent the last 20 minutes shaking at the door. Held only loosely on the internal catch, slight play had allowed the outside bolt to work gently back into place, perhaps by only the smallest amount. But it was enough to trap me inside; I was a prisoner.

I spent the next ten minutes trying to rattle the bolt back, while grim humour gave way to disbelief. There were no other entrances save for a small sealed vent in the roof, and no hinged windows. The door, now fast because of the bolt outside, refused to budge. True, I might have broken through the door but, once it was gone, the wind would come raging in unchecked and probably lift off the entire roof. Although I was less than 20 yards from the house, no sound I could make would be heard above the noise of the gale. What was more, after doing the rounds I'd planned to go straight into the garage to start work on the car, so would probably not be missed for at least another couple of hours. As I pondered my predicament, the wind shrieked as though with delight, pummelling the walls and hammering on the door.

Some minutes later, through the corrugated perspex, I saw a quick movement in the garden outside. I realised at once what was happening, and knew it was my only chance. Inside the house, one of the dogs – probably old Zoe – had stirred from beside the fire. Some of the others would have pretended not to notice, while the rest slept on, oblivious. But they all knew the rule: once one needed to go out, the rest would be sent regardless. So they would have been roused, chivvied and cajoled – especially Gelly, who always pretended to be deaf, invisible or both, particularly when the weather was bad. They would be shepherded into the front porch, and the inner door would be closed behind them, like an airlock, before the outer door was opened to the elements.

At that point, eight shivering bundles of whippet, all crowding together until the last possible second, would fire out of the doorway as though from a cannon. They would fly in all directions around the house to find a sheltered spot, before skidding to a halt moments later back outside the door, piling in like jets onto a carrier deck. Safely back inside, once admitted beyond the sanctuary of the inner door, they would race to get first position on their bed of sheepskin rugs beside the fire, before finally settling back down.

The movement I had seen, out there among the hammering tussocks and the shrubs, was the first of those highly sprung projectiles ricocheting around the garden – probably Oxo, the fittest and fastest and always first past the post. Next came a white blob of head that could only be Tot, so named because she was only four ounces at birth, but born to follow her big sister regardless, even in the teeth of every gale.

I called out to them, rapping on the door and waving to get their attention. I knew that if I could get them to come over and bark, thinking I was playing, their noise would bring my wife to the window. The two of them dashed forward into the wind, giving one or two playful woofs, before retreating, keen to turn and run back indoors. I had to keep them at it. There were other shapes now, milling around, and although I couldn't discern them clearly, I knew their movements. Along came Skye, boisterous and bulldozing in, keen to see what all the fuss was about but anxious not to be outdone in the race back. Then came Pip headlong around the corner as she collided into the others, giving one quick yap before she'd had enough. Gelly was bouncing around like a jack-in-the-box. I had a brief glimpse of Zoe at the back; she shivered in the wind, not wanting to be outside. Next came Fred, who dashed up as sinuous as a weasel hopping around on the grass.

 91

And then came Penny, reliably ambling up. Steady and steadfast, with her head down in the wind, she sailed along like some stately Victorian matron to see where I was and what all the fuss was about.

The moment they were all together, I knew there would be only one chance. If only I could get them started, the odds were that pack instinct would take over and make it self-sustaining. Frantically I started to coax, calling, cajoling and inciting them to bark wildly. And they did. For about 30 seconds it became one mad chorus of yapping pandemonium. Out there in the walled garden a pack of whippets pranced, barked and bounced around, dancing and dipping in the wild wind.

I peered through the perspex, desperate to see some sign of life within the house. Nothing.

Zoe was the first to disappear, followed closely by Pip and Gelly. Skye came back once, then, seeing that I was okay, remembered there was a race to the front door. Oxo and Tot scrapped a little longer, then, disappointed that I wasn't joining in, turned for home. Fred, always a slip of a lad, to his credit bounced over again to see what he could do, but the look on his face said quite plainly that he'd had more than he could take. He was thin-skinned and had no coat, and 50 knots of wind carried too keen a chill.

Only Penny remained, sitting patiently on the grass and looking at me. I spoke to her, explaining what had happened and what I needed her to do. She began barking again, her distinctive voice welling up deep and gravelly. I kept on encouraging her, and all the while she sat there, impervious to the howling gale fighting to drown out the sound. Only once did she begin to falter, but by then the desperation in my own voice must have spurred her on. She sat down again on the grass and barked endlessly, defying the wind with a bark that said she would not be moved until help arrived. A figure finally appeared behind her, coming from the house. And so my trap was sprung.

Back inside the warm comfort of the house with Pen and the others, I thanked her with real and heartfelt gratitude. I've always believed that animals really respond not just when you talk to them but when you treat them as individuals. Open and honest affection is the most genuine form of communication.

Of course Penny never made a fuss, but she knew what she'd done. Now, looking back on that day, a lifetime ago, I think that she may have felt that helping to release me from captivity was just her way of returning the favour.

Gary Wright
London
England

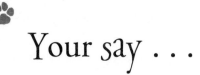

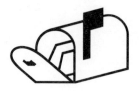

Your say . . .

Here at SMARTER than JACK we love reading the mail we receive from people who have been involved with our books. This mail includes letters both from contributors and readers and from the animal welfare charities that have benefited. We thought we would share with you excerpts from some of the letters that really touched our hearts.

'I already enjoy the entertaining and clever stories about smart animals emailed to me each week, and plan to write further stories that may appear in future SMARTER than JACK books.

I hope this dog book proves as successful as your previous series and look forward to reading it.'

Louisa, Scotland

'It will be a fitting tribute to my wonderful friend who was stolen nearly three years ago (on election night 2002). He was an inspiration in loyalty and devotion and I still miss him badly. It is not knowing where he is or who took him and what might have happened – or whether he is still "out there" – which makes his loss more acute. However, I am delighted that he will "live on" through this book.'

Heather, New Zealand

'I enjoyed the last edition [of SMARTER than JACK], as did my friends for whom I provided copies as Christmas presents.'

Lyn, Canada

'I am sure that the SMARTER than JACK books are a very positive influence in encouraging public concern about and respect for all animals and living creatures.'

Marjorie, Canada

'We're very excited about Fillipa's story being included, and really hope that the book will sell well and be of great benefit to the "rescues". Fillipa was an unwanted show dog, and we've also had another retired show dog and a "rescue" – all Cavaliers – so "rescue/recycling" is very close to our hearts.'

Nicki, Scotland

'I love your books and look forward to reading many more. A wonderful way to raise money for animal welfare. Great stuff!'

Faye, New Zealand

'Dear friends,
    In December I purchased a SMARTER than JACK book.
    I started to read it and my husband became most annoyed, complaining that we had spent so much money on a vacation to New Zealand and all I wanted to do was read a book. It wasn't just any book, it was your book! I love it! Keep up the wonderful work!'

Vera, Australia

'It was a great surprise and pleasure for me to hear from you that my story had been chosen. Thank you very much and I wish you all the best for this extraordinary project.'

Leonie, Germany

95

'I am so happy to have my story chosen to be published along with many others in the upcoming edition of SMARTER than JACK.'

Vanessa, Australia

'We think the SMARTER than JACK programme and reading materials are an important part of humane education, which is the only way we will stop the problems of pet overpopulation and cruelty to animals. The books are great for children and we plan to promote them when we go out on "tour" – to the local mall and to other community events.'

Lisa Beyer, Vice President and Publicity Chair
Animal Rescue Foundation, Inc.

Lisa and Anthea of SMARTER than JACK
enjoy some letters

96

7

Smart dogs lend a paw

Kinta and Leo – two very smart kelpies

A natural herder puts her skill to good use

The kelpie is one of the smartest breeds of dog in the world – and we are the very biased owners of two of them! Our chocolate kelpie Kinta is five years old and our red kelpie Leo is three.

Leo was an RSPCA adoptee and 16 weeks old when we brought him home. He was a real terror of a pup, with a lot of bad habits and way too smart for his own good!

He always knew when he had done something wrong and would run underneath our house and hide. The space was too small for us to get into to chase him out. One day, my husband Paul decided to train Kinta to run underneath the house and chase him out. As kelpies are natural herders we thought she was perfect for the job.

She caught on fast and whenever we said 'Kinta, get Leo' she would run under the house and bring him out to us to face the music. Even though Leo is all grown up and thankfully now very well behaved, this skill still comes in very handy at bath time, vet time, worming time and travel time. We are currently in the process of teaching Kinta to round up our cat in the same way, but I don't know how successful this will be!

Kinta also dutifully gathers up her toys from around the yard when Paul gets the lawnmower out.

People often comment that having two kelpies must be a lot of work. While we admit that they do need a lot of exercise and mental stimulation, we don't mind. To us, there is nothing more rewarding than the companionship, love and interaction we receive from our two very smart, very charismatic dogs. Sometimes we have to remember that they are, in fact, dogs and not people!

We wouldn't have it any other way.

Kristina Stewart
Bundaberg, Queensland
Australia

Write to me ... ✉
email Kristina at:
fordkris@yahoo.com

Peter the great

Dogs like to bring things home. Odd things, like other people's shoes, bits of rope or even the rotting carcasses of dead animals. Peter, our fox terrier, frequently brought home these little treasures, and I am firmly convinced he thought he was providing for his family.

He went everywhere with me – fishing, swimming, hiking up hills at the foot of the Selkirk Mountains in British Columbia. And if the door was left open a split second too long, he would follow me to school.

One day he sneaked out when my mother went to hang up the washing. With a big load of sheets and towels in her arms, she didn't see him dart under her feet and out the door. He'd done this before, and come home with people's odd shoes, once even an umbrella more than twice his size. It was embarrassing having to phone our neighbours to ask if they were missing a running shoe or a sandal. Peter's ears drooped when we didn't show enthusiasm over his gift.

One day I had choir practice after school and didn't get home until late. Peter was at the door waiting for me, a long dish beside him on the stoop.

At first I thought my mother had put the dish outside for some reason. But the gleam in Peter's eyes, the tail-wagging and tongue-lolling smile, gave the game away.

'What is it this time, boy?' I groaned. I could just hear the neighbours laughing; Peter's adventures had become legendary. If anyone missed a shoe these days, they didn't look far for it. They called us.

It was a wide, shallow dish of rice pudding, untouched and still warm. Someone must have put it out on their porch to cool off.

'How did you do that, Peter?' It wasn't a light dish – in fact, it was as long as he was, and the pudding was heavy. He must have somehow dragged it along the street or back alley. It was amazing that no one had seen him. I carried it into the house, a happy dog prancing at my side.

We called everyone nearby. No one was missing a rice pudding. We never did find out who it belonged to; no one had seen a small dog dragging an enormous dish around. So waste not, want not. It was delicious, almost as good as Mum's own. 'A little heavy on the cinnamon,' my father announced, but cleaned up his share anyway.

Peter hadn't eaten any himself, and ignored the spoonful we plopped into his dish. But he stuck his little chest out as far as it could go, and virtually bounced as he trotted around the house that night. He may not have brought home the bacon, but he'd finally brought home something we liked.

Sharman Horwood
Seoul
South Korea

Write to me ... ✉
email Sharman
sharmanh2004@yahoo.ca

Sharman Horwood is a Canadian writer living in Seoul, South Korea.

A canine real estate agent

It is widely recognised that moving house is the next most stressful experience to a marriage break-up or bereavement. One of the most traumatic and disheartening aspects is the process of showing prospective buyers around your house.

This onerous task was lifted from us in an unexpected way.

During the showing round our Ibizan hound/whippet cross Trefle would accompany us, presumably noting how it was done. One day she 'took over' the task, preceding the procession and giving a gentle nudge to the prospective buyers if they lingered too long in one room.

Trefle made selling the house a pleasure

She would lead them into each room and up the two flights of stairs in a precise order. We soon left it to her, for the buyers were amazed and intrigued by their unusual guide. I'd hear them say, 'Look, she wants us to go that way now' or 'She is telling us to go up the stairs'. Then she would conduct them around the garden and outbuildings, hustling them round any shabby areas and lingering in the better ones.

Needless to say, the procedure became a pleasure rather than a chore, and before long we started to get offers which they were obliged to give to us rather than Trefle.

Sadly, we lost her when she was 11, so when we next want to move we won't have this help, as we don't think any of our present dogs will undertake the role. Trefle was never asked or trained to

 101

do it; she seemed to sense that we didn't like the task and willingly volunteered her services. She was perceptive and seemed to know our inner thoughts.

Valerie and Gillian Rogers
Powys
Wales

Write to us ... ✉
Miss Valerie or Gillian Rogers
Cloverlands Museum
Pen-Y-Sarn, Waen Fach
Llansantffraid-Y-M
Powys, Wales
SY 22 6TH
United Kingdom

Silver's passion was herding animals

Silver was a great help on the farm

Ranching on a farm south of Esther, Alberta were Ray and Doreen Trevor and their son Dennis. They grew grain and had cattle and chickens.

One day Ray went to an auction sale. He came home with a skinny silver-coloured Australian blue heeler dog, who was soon named Silver. He was a very intelligent dog in many ways.

While eating dinner one day shortly after they bought him, they heard some barking coming from the barnyard. Dennis went to see what was happening. He returned and said, 'Dad and Mom, come see what Silver is doing.'

It was fall and they had weaned the calves. They were normally in a small corral, but that morning they had been let out into a larger corral. Silver was rounding them up and putting them back into the small corral. Then he turned and looked at the family with a smile and a look on his face that seemed to say, *There, they are back in the corral.* He looked so proud.

Doreen had chickens. They were forever coming into the yard and she would shoo them out. Barn cats and gophers also came into the yard. Silver had no love for these animals, so he kept the yard clear.

In the spring Doreen's chickens had chicks, which she kept in a small building. As they grew older she let them out to eat green grass. Silver tried rounding them up and putting them back into their building. He found out they were not as easy to herd as cattle. A couple of the chicks didn't make it back – he was a bit too severe. Silver soon learned this was not one of his jobs.

His passion was herding animals. It was very easy to get the cattle into the corral, as once they saw Silver they knew where to go. He was great at loading cows and bulls into a truck.

 103

Ray and Doreen went on a holiday. When they phoned home, Dennis said that everything was fine and that he and Silver had vaccinated the cows and given them vitamin A.

'How did you do that?' Doreen asked.

Dennis said, 'We got the cows into the corral. Silver stood at the gate and let one out at a time.' As soon as Dennis finished with one cow, Silver would let another one out. They were soon finished.

Silver loved to be busy all the time. It got so that there wasn't much for him to do, so he took to chasing vehicles. Once when Dennis was going out of the yard, he and Silver collided and that was the end of Silver. What a sad day that was! They lost their dear smart dog but have many happy memories of him.

Doreen Trevor
Oyen, Alberta
Canada

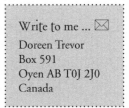

Write to me ... ✉
Doreen Trevor
Box 591
Oyen AB T0J 2J0
Canada

Tess – my treasure

My whippet cross is called Tess but I call her my treasure as she is so helpful around the house and such a good companion. She cheers me up.

If we're going out for a walk she will pick up my discarded shoes and give them to me. When we return she fetches my house shoes. This is such a welcome little gesture, because I look after my elderly mum all the time but there's no one to look after me – except Tess.

When I've had back trouble, she has patiently pulled the washing out of the machine and given it to me. If my mum drops things she picks them up for her. If I carry a cup and saucer through to the

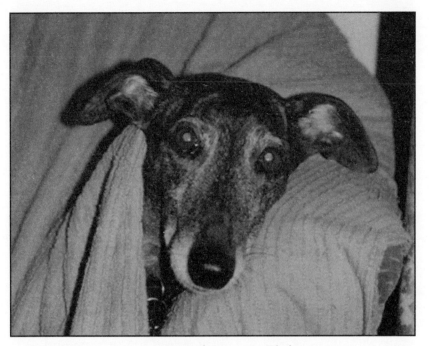

Tess is wonderful at helping around the house

kitchen and the teaspoon falls to the floor, she comes to pick it up for me, mostly without being asked. In fact, if she hears me drop anything she'll come and pick it up.

I have tied a cord to doors so she can pull them open or shut if I ask her to. She seems to listen to what I'm doing, and if I'm in the kitchen preparing vegetables she seems able to differentiate between my peeling potatoes or carrots. If it's potatoes she stays put in her chair (she doesn't eat potatoes) and if it's carrots she comes through to the kitchen for carrot treats. I can only assume she's learned that peeling carrots uses lengthier strokes than potatoes, or maybe it's because I scrub the carrots before I peel them.

If anything is difficult for me to reach, or I don't want to bend because my back is painful, she will get it for me. I have to confess, though, that this help doesn't come for free. I have to pay her with her special biscuit treats. No doubt this is why she is obliging, but it's all very helpful and much appreciated. One can't be sad when she's around.

What a treasure she is, and to think she was a stray who picked all these things up so easily.

Mrs C Campbell
North Lincolnshire
England

A cattle dog found 'stock' to herd

My parents acquired a pair of bantam chickens to combat an infestation of earwigs.

The rooster's morning voice was as powerful as that of a bird three times his size. Betty Boop, as we called the hen, was an animated pile of black feathers with only her toes showing. They patrolled the yard and garden during the day, ignoring the cat and dog and staying out of the surrounding woods. At night they slept safely in a small coop.

My parents also had a dog called Pandy, who had been mine until I left home. I was told she was an Australian cattle dog. I don't know if her mother had cattle to herd, but we had none. She was as big as a medium-sized collie, and was gentle and loving.

I went home for a summer visit about two years later and saw Betty Boop in the backyard with a flock of black chicks, each no bigger than a dandelion seed head. Normally a very fussy mother, Betty seemed unworried by the big black dog close by. When I looked closer, I could see that as the bantam led her chicks Pandy was gently nosing the wandering bits of fluff back into the flock.

The herder dog had finally found something to herd.

Pegeen McAskill
New Westminster, British Columbia
Canada

'The rope's yours, Cherry Cola'

We have six German shepherds ranging in age from six years to ten months. They get on very well except for the odd quarrel.

One day the two youngest pups were having a game of tug of war with a knotted rope, and for once in her life Cherry Cola was winning against her much stronger cousin Rudi. She managed to get control of the rope and paraded around the yard with it.

Rudi pinned her down, and an older female dog apparently decided to get in on the act and help him out. By the time I managed to stop them, she was shaken up and limping. I screamed at Rudi and the older female, and the other dogs sensed my anger and backed away.

All except the oldest male, Khan, the pack leader. He went to the rope, which was about 30 yards away, picked it up and carried it to Cherry Cola. He placed it at her feet and then came to sit next to me.

Gentiana Mansfield
Taree, New South Wales
Australia

 107

How can I stop little Miss Houdini?

My boxer, aptly named Angel, is the world's most amazing escape artist. Our house is fully fenced, seemingly totally secure, surrounded by two metre high solid wood. Yet three days out of five, when I get home from work Angel has escaped. We live in a nice quiet street and Angel is always waiting for me – outside the gate – when I get home. I'm sure she has a big grin on her face. I just don't have the heart to tell her off. What can I do to keep her secure?

Can you offer any advice? Contact us at SMARTER than JACK.

How can I choose a smart puppy?

I'm looking for a puppy to join our family. How do I spot a really smart one? The last dog we had certainly wouldn't have made it into any smart animal book!

So what things should I look for? Should I go for the quiet one, the playful one, the bossy one? Any help is most appreciated! I'm not fussed about what kind of dog we get, so long as it's not too big and doesn't slobber everywhere.

Can you offer any advice? Contact us at SMARTER than JACK.

8

Smart dogs make us wonder

Bobby knew when I was coming home

Bobby was a collie cross who came from the Dogs' Home and became a much loved companion.

I went to work, but my husband was ill and home all day. Every day when I came home, Bobby was in the porch watching for me. He would ask for the door to be opened when my husband judged I was about halfway home.

Some days I'd decide to go shopping first. At these times he would not ask to go out, but when I was about halfway home, perhaps an hour and half later, he'd want to go out and wait for me. He was never wrong and we wondered how he knew. It makes me wonder if animals have senses beyond our own which enable them to have a unique conception of events.

Mrs Joyce Taylor
Bristol
England

Write to me ...
email Joyce at:
pegotty2000@tiscali.co.uk

Would you open that door for me, please?

We have two female basset hounds, about ten years old.

Our daughter's room is downstairs and just needs a push to open it; the door handle doesn't need to be turned. Phoebe has no trouble opening the door but Bailey cannot manage it yet.

One day Bailey went downstairs and sat outside Liz's bedroom door for quite a while. Eventually she must have got fed up, and came upstairs again. Somehow she communicated something to Phoebe, for she immediately trotted downstairs, put her head down and barged the door open. She then stood aside and looked up at Bailey, as much as to say, *There you are, Sis, I've opened it for you.* Bailey trotted downstairs and into the bedroom. My daughter was having a snack there, hence Bailey's interest.

How did she communicate this to Phoebe, who did not see her sitting downstairs? There was nothing obvious going on between them, but somehow Phoebe got the message.

Jean Lang
Wellington
New Zealand

Come on, surely you recognise me?

My neighbour Helen had a Labrador puppy, and whenever we visited, James was beside himself to see me. Even when he grew up he had to be restrained from bowling me over, and when Helen and I sat on the grass chatting, he'd try to come as close as possible and sit on my lap. It was a mystery to us as to why I seemed to be his favourite person.

We both eventually moved away. Eight years later, I was invited to a luncheon attended by about 20 other people.

A Labrador greeted me as soon as I stepped through the door. It wagged its tail and nudged my hands. I petted him, murmured, 'Good boy' and moved on but the dog kept following me, wanting attention.

'I didn't know you had a Labrador,' I said to my hostess.

'No, he isn't mine. I'm looking after him for my neighbour Helen while she's on holiday.'

I felt stupid and also guilty for not recognising my old friend. He, smart dog, knew instantly who I was.

Louise Buurmans
Waikanae Beach
New Zealand

Benji knows when to expect my husband

Benji, our Yorkie, has many talents. Among them is knowing when my husband is returning home.

He can be out in the car, or on the train, but Benji looks through the window exactly 15 minutes before he arrives home. He can also tell when it's precisely 9 pm each evening, and goes upstairs to bed.

He sorts out his food in the bowl, removing the larger bits of biscuits, but replaces them tidily when he's finished. When my son's Border collie visits, Benji stands back halfway through his meal and saves half for her. How many dogs would share a meal? Sometimes he'll bring her a chew that he's hidden.

Mrs D Brookfield
Sheffield, South Yorkshire
England

How did he know?

Every Thursday evening when the man came to deliver the football pools coupon, our golden spaniel Ben used to sit by the front door, waiting for him.

The man would give the dog a spare coupon to keep, and he'd bring it indoors. Ben never sat by that door in the hall any other evening. How did he know when it was Thursday?

Mrs Joan Reason
Billericay, Essex
England

What was he looking at?

Angus is a West Highland white terrier with an unusual awareness of suffering in other dogs.

He met my shih-tzu Oggie in Winchester when Oggie was 13 and Angus three. Soon after Oggie's seventeenth birthday he went to stay for a night at Angus's home. When I arrived to collect him, he got to his feet rather stiffly, upon which Angus jumped down from the sofa and nosed his hind leg and under his thigh with apparent concern, looking up to draw the attention of his owner. We remarked upon it at the time.

Oggie was diagnosed with kidney failure not long afterwards. We were expecting Angus for a visit while his owner Diana had an operation. It seemed a bad time to take on another dog but in fact it proved a godsend. From the moment he arrived, Angus became Oggie's guardian, watching over him and providing him with the friendship of his own kind.

One evening, when Oggie was in the garden on his own, I was alerted by Angus springing up and running to the door. Oggie had

Does Angus have a sixth sense?

had a stroke, and was lying with a paralysed left foreleg. I carried him indoors and laid him on the carpet, massaging his back and leg to see if it would ease him.

Angus was beside me, all his attention fixed on his friend. Suddenly he seized Oggie's 'armpit' in his jaws, gave the paralysed leg two or three vigorous jerks, then stood back and looked into his face. I stopped and watched him, with a feeling of awe. Angus repeated the 'operation' three or four times, each time peering into Oggie's face for a response, until he was obliged to stand back, apparently baffled.

The time had come to have Oggie put to sleep. The vet was booked for the next day, and Angus and I sat up all night to watch over our friend. For much of the time he slept on his cushion, while Angus settled on an armchair beside him, growling whenever I approached. When I carried Oggie outside to empty his bladder, Angus muscled in, pushing up along his paralysed left side and standing close against him to keep him upright and prevent him falling over, even though I was supporting Oggie on my own. He was acting quite independently of me.

When the vet arrived, Angus barked so insistently he had to be shut in the next room. Oggie had his final injection lying on my lap, and we laid him on his cushion by the hearth.

By the time the vet had left, Angus was barking again. As soon as the door was open he rushed in, leaping in pursuit of something nearer the ceiling than the floor. He ran part-way up the stairs, reaching out for it with his paw, then pranced about on the furniture, leaping up to catch what was clearly flying there before his eyes. In his progress, he ran around Oggie without even seeing him, did a double take, stopped and briefly sniffed his head, before dismissing the body in favour of the far more real vision only he could see.

We watched in silent amazement, each of us feeling we had been granted a special privilege. We wondered if he could be chasing a flying insect, but there was nothing of the kind. Besides, Angus behaves quite differently with flies, jumping about on the floor and snapping his jaws. It seemed that his objective when he came into the room was his friend and nothing else.

Only later, when Oggie was lying in his casket, did Angus settle quietly beside him. He showed no signs of grief or of missing Oggie, either then or later. But the next day I heard a curious sound, and glanced into the room to find him standing before the hearth with his gaze fixed above the fireguard. He was poised and all attention, listening avidly and then 'speaking' in a curious voice quite different from his usual sounds. The listening and speaking were repeated two or three times. Finally his eyes went upward, as if whatever held his attention had risen out of sight. He became his usual self again and walked away.

This was in May 2003. More recently, when I was looking after him again, I took him to the place where Oggie is buried. He stood by the grave and barked 'fit to wake the dead', looking at me pointedly all the time. Occasionally he took a turn around the burial ground, exploring in companionable silence, but each time he returned to the grave he resumed his fanfare.

Patricia Johnson
Brentwood, Essex
England

Write to me ... ✉
email Patricia at
strophalos@aol.com

Psychic dog

I rescued Zappa, a cross-bred mini fox terrier bitch, from the pound, but she didn't make herself popular. She was too ready to snap at ankles, making no discrimination between family and friends. Even Grandma was a victim. Still, my dog and I were close ... but our bonds were even stronger than I thought.

As a young man, I often came home at the oddest hours and never to any regular schedule. My family never knew when to expect me, and as I had a pretty hectic social life I'd never commit to a timetable of any sort. I'd happily deviate to visit friends on a whim, arriving late for dinner or early for breakfast.

However, there was one indicator of my impending arrival: my faithful dog Zappa. During the daytime she'd climb onto the narrow window ledge in the lounge room and start pining and crying for me. Anyone at home would know I could be expected to arrive within a few minutes. It was impossible for my dog to hear my car from a few minutes away in a built-up suburban area, and my car was a very common one, a late model that was no noisier than any others in the '70s.

Of course, I relate this story as a third person since my family members were the only ones to witness what happened. But Zappa's accuracy was uncanny. Call it coincidence, but she was so reliable that my family depended on her without fail to announce my arrival.

Casey Herman
Noble Park, Victoria
Australia

Write to me ... ✉
email Casey at:
casey@twistedirony.com

Even dogs fall in love

PD was a small black and tan dog who'd had a horrid life. He was kept in a cupboard until he was sold to a woman who put him in a dark basement, tied to a post. Every now and then, the light went on and kids came downstairs to tease and hurt him.

He was eventually rescued and lived happily for the next eight years. His nature was not sweet. He was crabby to other animals and even to the person he loved best.

When he was about ten, a silky-furred red dog came to live at his home. Foxy had a gentle nature and was just his size. If dogs can fall in love, those two fell in love at once. They lay together, ate together and washed each other's faces and ears. PD was never cross or crabby with Foxy.

When PD died of lung cancer four years later, Foxy was bereft. She sat on the stairs watching the door, and would go to his bed and work the bedclothes over, apparently searching for him. She hardly ate and lost interest in her usual activities.

Before he died, an artist had begun a portrait of PD's head. When the picture was brought home, three months after his death, we stood it on the ground so Foxy could see it. Her tail wagging, she jumped off the couch, ran to it and sniffed it all over. Then she checked it out from the back. Her tail and ears drooped and she went away to lie down. Had she realised it wasn't him? After that day, she gave up looking for him and resumed her normal life.

We got another small dog in the hopes of filling the gap but it didn't work. I don't think she will ever fall in love again.

Jane McIntyre
Whitehorse, Yukon
Canada

Write to me ...

Jane McIntyre
109 Rainbow Road
Whitehorse YT Y1A 3X3
Canada

A friend in need

Much to his disgust, my dad received a white kitten for his birthday. He had a black exclamation mark between his ears, and we named him Sadge. Our golden Labrador Mona adored the kitten, and they would play-fight all the time.

Fast forward three years, and Sadgie went missing. We live in the Riverland, South Australia and there are many brown snakes in summer. We were all worried, particularly Mona.

After a week we were sure Sadgie had met his final match, and he had. Mona found him. She brought him up to the pathway where Mum walked every morning. We buried him that morning, and when we'd finished saying our goodbyes, Mona disappeared.

She came back with one of her bones. She had refused to eat it the night before, and now she put it alongside Sadgie's grave and gave it a light covering of sand.

 117

Mona wouldn't eat for several days. We went to the local fodder shop and found her a new friend. She became as good as new again, but from time to time she would go and lie beside Sadgie, as if to say he wasn't forgotten.

Samantha Maywald
Waikerie, South Australia

How did Wally know when I didn't need the paper?

Back in 1980, we purchased a Lhasa apso pup and named him Wally.

At the time, I owned a small bus service and occasionally the railways department would charter my buses to run in lieu of trains while they worked on the overhead wires. On these weekends I would buy my Sunday paper at an early-opening newsagent, then go home, throw the paper on a chair and go to bed.

The newsboys delivered the papers in a wheelbarrow and blew a whistle to let you know they were coming. Normally, Wally would come into my room and wake me long before I heard the whistle and I would be out the front waiting when the boy arrived. On the days that I brought the paper home early, he did not wake me. How did he know?

Terry Cole
Corrimal East, New South Wales
Australia

Mona never forgot her cat friend Sadge

How does she know?

My German shepherd Shelley and I always visited my parents, who lived in a hostel. She always led me to the door of their room and lay beside my mother's chair during our visits. When Shelley was two years old, my mother died.

I was passing the cemetery a month or so later and decided to visit my mother's grave. I said to Shelley, 'Where's Gran?' She went straight to my mother's grave and lay down beside it!

I later realised that there were fresh flowers on the grave and that they had been placed there by my father the day before. I believe Shelley followed his scent – but she certainly made the hair stand up on the back of my neck.

My father has since died and is buried with my mother, and Shelley still knows where their grave is, even though other graves now surround it. How does she know?

Can you offer any advice? Contact us at SMARTER than JACK.

9

Smart dogs take care of others

Holly's gentle touch

Holly, my 'rescue' dog, was very boisterous and always seemed to be running off. But when I had a major operation on my knee she became my best friend.

It was as though she knew she had to be gentle with me. When I came out of the hospital, instead of the usual welcome which would have literally swept me off my feet, she gently licked my hand and sat next to me. When I was down she would lick the tears on my face and appear to comfort me. If I was by myself, she would stay by my side, never leaving me, as if she knew that I was more fragile than I'd been previously.

When I could walk without crutches she was still fantastic. Our walks were leisurely, not the running madness that they used to be. She wouldn't run off, she just walked next to me. The funny thing was, she was still exuberant with everyone else. It was as if she knew I wasn't the same.

Because she was normally so energetic, many people thought she was an overgrown puppy. But at the time when I needed her most, her caring, sensitive and intelligent side came into its own.

Zoë Cassidy
Coleby, Lincolnshire
England

 121

I trained Ben to be my ears

When Ben was only ten months old he was going to be put to sleep as his owners couldn't handle him. My daughter-in-law phoned to ask me if I could save his life.

In she came with a young springer spaniel. I thought, 'No wonder they couldn't handle him', as it takes a lot of patience to look after a springer. They are boisterous and into everything. Ben came and lay down at my feet, and the funny thing was that every time they told me about his behaviour he'd look up at me as if to say, *Not true*. So I kept him.

As I'm deaf and only partially sighted, I first trained him to be my ears. It's his job to tell me when the doorbell rings. He also tells me when the smoke alarm goes off. I cannot see too well now, so my son made a harness for him. Ben takes me around town to do my shopping, and has even been in a lift. He's so clever he even tells me when it's time to have my hourly eye drops. He has more than paid for his keep and has even won a prize for being the most friendly dog in the pet show.

Bob Hewitson
Grimsby, North East Lincolnshire
England

Bonnie was Gordon's faithful guardian

Bonnie, a boxer, was bred as a show dog but when she broke her leg as a pup she became a 'rescue' dog instead. When we got her she was so nervous she didn't know how to play, and if we tried to pet her she would back away.

My husband's aunt and uncle died suddenly within a month of each other, leaving their son Gordon, who suffered from epilepsy and Down's syndrome, with no one to care for him. My husband and I decided we could do it, and Gordon came to live with us.

At the time, Gordon was having at least ten seizures a day. The first day he was with us, Bonnie sat at his feet and kept lifting her paw to him. Gordon was a bit wary of dogs so we told her to come away but she wouldn't.

We thought she was triggering his seizures, but in fact Bonnie was warning us before they actually happened. It took us about a week to realise this. We were flabbergasted and over the moon.

We had a security camera trained on Gordon while he slept, and alarms on his bedroom door so we'd hear him trying to get out of his

Bonnie could predict Gordon's seizures

 123

room. This would be dangerous as we have stairs and Gordon could not come downstairs by himself. One morning my husband was in the kitchen when he saw Bonnie dash upstairs. He ran after her, to see her fly into Gordon's room and onto his bed. He was having a seizure; we could neither hear nor see it but Bonne had sensed it and was alerting us. She taught Gordon that he had no need to be scared of her, and he loved to cuddle her.

Bonnie gave birth to a litter of eight in August 2002. We asked Gordon to pick one to have his name, and he chose a white pup to be named Flash Gordon.

Gordon suddenly died in his sleep later that month. He was only 23 and we were devastated.

We had people wanting to buy Flash Gordon but I kept saying no. I just felt it had to be someone really special and I was right. We were contacted by a minister of the church who had emigrated from America. He didn't have much money but could offer Flash an excellent home with all the love he could handle. Tony and his family were everything I was looking for. Flash Gordon is now with them, and his nickname is Gringo.

Bonnie is still just as attentive. My sister was sleeping in my house and snoring quite loudly. She stopped for an instant and Bonnie was right over her, checking she was okay.

Yvonne Finnigan
Peebles
Scotland

Write to me ... ✉
email Yvonne at:
finnigan31@btinternet.com

Amy works as a furry therapist

These days, chihuahuas are most often seen in the handbags of trendy young ladies. They've become something of a must-have fashion accessory. This is the story of one who is much more than that.

My daughter was only 11 when she came down with ME. It started with a dose of the flu and she just never got better. Not only did she feel exhausted most of the time, but almost constant headaches, painful glands, sore muscles and occasional feverishness added to her misery. Going to school was out of the question and she lost contact with her friends. At night the exhaustion would reach such a peak that she became utterly distraught, and yet she often couldn't get to sleep and began to suffer from night terrors. The only solution seemed to be to move her into our bedroom so she could sleep within a comforting arm's reach of her mum.

By the following spring, just over a year since her illness began, she was able to go to school for one or two lessons per day but, as an only child, still spent much of her time alone. She had often begged us to get her a chihuahua, her favourite dog breed, but since we already had two dogs we'd resisted. Now it began to make sense.

We found a puppy through the Kennel Club website and drove to Herne Bay to pick her up from the breeder. She hid behind the fridge and had to be dragged out, but her sweet features sold her to us and we took her home, to my daughter's delight. She called her Amy.

The first thing Amy did for my daughter was to give her, overnight, the confidence to sleep in her own room again after over a year of sleeping next to our bed. To us, this was a huge step and a great relief.

Amy soon played happily with our English bull terrier cross and tried to charm our rather aloof German shepherd. She and my daughter became inseparable companions, and I have marvelled at

 125

the wisdom with which Amy recognised that my daughter was her 'special person' even though she got quite a lot of attention from both me and my husband.

I'm convinced that Amy has helped to keep my daughter free from the depression that afflicts so many with ME. AYME (Association of Young People with ME) acknowledges the benefits of pet ownership for young people isolated by this debilitating illness, and uses the term 'furry therapy'. Amy has proved to be a 'furry therapist' par excellence.

Mrs M Watson
London
England

A basket fit for friends

My Border collie Mocha has never been a dog who likes cats. Once, though, we had an old cat called Skling who would sleep in her basket on the floor all day long.

One morning my mum woke me up and we went into the dining room for breakfast. Mocha and Skling were in their own baskets, sleeping. I patted them both, said good morning and then got ready for school.

That afternoon when I got home I saw Mocha in her bed, and lying next to her was Skling. Mocha had let Skling share her bed. They were both sleeping happily.

The next morning I walked into the dining room and looked at the two baskets. In Mocha's big basket I saw Skling sleeping. I looked at Skling's small basket, and there trying to sleep was Mocha. Mocha had let Skling have her basket, even though she was too big to fit in Skling's basket.

A few days later, Skling died. We buried her in our garden next to our other cat's grave. Everyone was sad, but not as sad as Mocha. It was like she had lost her best friend. Mocha has never let a cat into her bed since.

Emilia Barr
Paekakariki
New Zealand

Beau became my mother's 'ears'

I once had a beautiful little white poodle named Beau. When he was three – beautifully trained and not a barker – my mother offered to babysit while I moved house.

Six weeks later Mum asked if she could keep him because he was such a loving companion and had become her 'ears'. I asked her what she meant, and she told me that within a few days he had realised she was (partially) deaf and, when she was in the kitchen or her bedroom, could not hear the telephone ring or a knock on the front door.

He would run to her, bark two or three times to get her attention, then walk to the telephone table or the door. I knew he was intelligent but this was something else! Of course, Mum kept him and had him for ten great years.

Beverley Evans
Sydney, New South Wales
Australia

Write to me ...
Beverley Evans
PO Box 4075
Castlecrag, Sydney
NSW 2068
Australia

Bonnie she was

I knew Bonnie#2 was special when I first saw her. She was about to play a major role in the biggest deception I've ever committed.

I gave Mom a puppy for Mother's Day 12 years ago. She was a pure-bred Kuvasz, one of those rare Hungarian sheepdogs with snow-white hair. They grow to be larger than golden retrievers. Mom called her Bonnie and we became quite attached to her.

Everything was great until Mom discovered protrusions coming from the puppy's belly. I assessed them to be multiple tiny hernias and arranged to take her to the breeder's vet. But she died on the operating table, having succumbed to a rare abdominal condition. The vet told me the breeder had agreed to pay the bill and had also offered another puppy as a replacement.

My problem was that Mom had already lost two family dogs in the past few months. I knew she would likely decline the new puppy.

I called the breeder, Darla Lofranco, and we concocted an elaborate scheme to avoid having to tell Mom that Bonnie had died.

Darla introduced me to Bonnie#2 and I knew she was special. In a breed known for their tenacious character (they were bred to fight off wolf packs preying on sheep) she was a sweet spirit. Any doubts over what I was about to do were forgotten after the first wet, sloppy kiss she planted on my cheek.

I told my parents that Bonnie would need three weeks to recuperate at the vet's and that I'd pick her up and bring her home. Mom had never asked to see the first Bonnie's official papers so I was certain she'd never notice the differences on Bonnie#2's. I prayed she wouldn't notice the puppies' tattoos were different. Bonnie#2 was born two weeks after Bonnie#1 so their size was similar.

I arrived home with the puppy, petrified that I'd be instantly found out. Bonnie#2 didn't really look much like Bonnie#1. If asked to explain, I'd attribute any differences to three weeks' growth during her alleged recuperation. I also used the scratches on Bonnie#2's belly (received from the sharp edge of a water bowl in her kennel) as perfect substitutions for the healing incisions Mom was bound to look for.

Bonnie roared straight into the living room, went to Mom and practically leaped onto her lap. Any guilt for my monkey business was fading rapidly.

In her entire life, she never bared a fang or even growled at a human. She was to become a celebrated charter member of St John's Ambulance Therapy Dogs in Canada.

Becoming a registered therapy dog isn't easy. The dogs are put through rigorous testing to ascertain their dependability around people. One snap, one growl at any point in their training or later in their careers and these dogs are drummed out. Bonnie's sweetness was unassailable.

Once, when she was promoting St John's Therapy Dogs at a crowded public function, my dad was surprised to hear her whimper in pain several times. He saw a man secretly pinching her ear and confronted him.

'I just wanted to see if she'd try to bite me,' the man said.

'She won't bite you, but I will!' Dad replied, his Irish eyes flashing.

Bonnie started out as a member of Therapy Dogs International when she was one. Mom had been training and socialising her with trips to a local nursing home since she was four months old.

She became a Canadian Kennel Club champion. And, for her part in helping founders Doreen and Jim Newell build the therapy dog programme in Canada, Mom was appointed an officer in St John's Ambulance Brigade, among other awards.

As a therapy dog Bonnie brought comfort and joy to many people's lives

The St John's Therapy Dogs programme has grown from an original eight dogs to more than 1500 dogs involved in communities across Canada.

Bonnie logged more than 700 hours visiting nursing homes, hospitals, shut-ins, Girl Guides, Sparks, Brownies and the developmentally handicapped. Mom found it particularly satisfying to see people's faces light up whenever she arrived with Bonnie in her familiar red harness and white St John's sash. Patients would come out of their shells and, after uttering hardly a word to anyone, would chat away to her.

Among Bonnie's career highlights was an invitation to a Canadian medical conference in 1993. She demonstrated to doctors the soothing and recuperative effects therapy dogs can have with patients.

In 1994 she posed with Toronto mayor Mel Lastman for a photo opportunity, which I consider to be a highlight of his career.

She was almost a movie star. She was recruited to be official backup to the Kuvasz starring in the movie *Homeward Bound II*. Alas, she wasn't called to perform on the big screen, but she did make it to the small screen. In 1993 she was the subject of a documentary on the value of therapy dogs, produced by the local cable TV station and distributed across Canada. For a dog, she accomplished a great deal in the community.

I finally confessed to my dad about my puppy-switching trickery. He was a little disappointed but never mentioned it again, and I suspect he thought I was right in thinking Mom wouldn't have accepted another puppy. I heard that he told Mom later but she's never said a word either. I think they just decided the Bonnie they had would always be Bonnie#1 – and she was.

Bonnie died at the age of 12, just a couple of days after Mother's Day.

Jim Phillips
Etobicoke, Ontario
Canada

Jim's mother Marlene Phillips sent us this story, which we adapted from an article first published in the *Toronto Sun*, so it can be assumed that she has definitely forgiven her son for his trickery. Thousands of dogs now visit nursing homes and hospitals throughout Canada.

A seizure alert dog

Bobo, a Cairn terrier cross, was tossed out of a moving car. My mother saw it happen.

She came home to our place, and helped raise hundreds of orphaned babies from squirrels to raccoons. She even helped take care of a puppy that was left for dead on the side of the road, by cleaning his eyes and wounds.

Bobo never left my side. Where I was, she was, especially when a new visitor arrived. But one night some of the children from our Sunday school came to visit. One child had a seizure disorder and Bobo would not leave the girl alone. She pawed at her, whined and tugged on her clothes. This was so out of character that I decided to put the dog to bed. She growled at me and, amazed, I left her alone.

The girl decided to sit down and pat Bobo. Moments later, she had a massive seizure. Bobo lay beside her, licking her face. When she woke up, Bobo left her side and came to me.

Bobo never went to anyone else again. She had turned out to be a natural seizure alert dog.

In loving memory of Bobo.

Cheryl Roberts
Chelsey, Ontario
Canada

I couldn't resist Patch's smile

My dog Patch isn't a hero. He hasn't saved anybody from drowning, or dialled 999 with his paw when the family was fast asleep and the curtains caught fire. He hasn't won a single doggy competition or prize. But to me he is wonderful. Patch smiles.

It's a great friendly smile that reminds me of a cartoon character out of a comic strip. Smiling is not being clever, of course, because he was born like that, with the ability to make me laugh and lighten the burden of everyday life. It's the way Patch uses his gift that I think is clever.

It was a grey winter morning and I didn't feel like getting up. I just wanted to lie in bed and forget about washing, dressing and getting ready for the day. Why bother to go through another day? What was the point? That's how I was feeling – down, lazy and sorry for myself. I'll stay here all day, I thought.

But someone had other plans. Patch jumped on the bed and licked my face. I could almost hear his thoughts: *Come on, it's time for my walk, what's wrong with you?* Running in the field and playing with his favourite ball had been our morning routine for years and he knew we were late that day. When his licking attempts failed to raise me from the bed, he pawed me gently, trying to lift the blanket off me. I still wouldn't move.

So Patch smiled. Nobody can resist a smiling dog, and that day Patch produced his best ever. I smiled back. Then I started laughing and my gloomy mood melted like icicles in the sun. 'Okay, you win. Let's go and play and say good morning to the world!'

Patch had worked his magic on me. Without words, my little dog had managed to change my apathy into a renewed zest for life, reminding me that life is short and there is no time for self-indulgence. To me, this is being clever.

Franca James
Oakhurst, Swindon, Wiltshire
England

Flint – my new ears

Five years ago I was a sad, unwell and depressed human being. Sad, because I had lost my dog, my dear companion. Unwell, because my business over the previous ten years, when I'd been working in all weathers, had taken its toll on my health.

I was also depressed, because my hearing had become much worse. I felt as though I was in a void. Because I was no longer working I wasn't meeting people, and without a dog I didn't get out as much. My family and friends had been supportive but I needed someone to turn to.

Flint came into my life when I needed her most. Her eyes look at me with the devotion and loyalty that is part of our bonding. Her head turns slightly when she knows I need her, and her paw is my touch to the world around me. Her ears are my ears, and she doesn't let me out of her sight.

Flint has been like a door opening to a new life, and together we're going forward. It's a world where people now stop to speak, and I stand tall to tell how my life has changed.

My wife Lin and I go to groups and schools to talk about hearing dogs for deaf people, to help raise funds to train more dogs. Flint is a wonderful example of a hearing dog, and she is so placid and friendly. She goes everywhere I go, and is well known in the audiology department of the local hospital. She sits patiently, sometimes for hours, in the dentist's and doctor's waiting rooms. When we walk in the town where we live we're constantly stopped, and she also has her friends in the park.

I lost confidence when I was on my own, and wouldn't even attend lip-reading classes without my wife. Lin still works, so now Flint accompanies me, and it is to her that I owe my regained confidence.

© Tim Flach

Mike and Flint

Flint wakes me each morning with the clock alarm and, instead of the dread I used to feel at the prospect of trying to get through the day, I now look forward to the hours ahead. I have a friend who is invaluable in my day-to-day existence.

Flint was rescued by the Southampton RSPCA when she was eight weeks old. We came together after she was trained, at a year old. About 75 per cent of hearing dogs are 'rescue' dogs, which to me is very special. An unwanted dog is trained to lead a useful life, thus changing a person's life and ending their isolation.

I have a yearly visit – or more if required – from a hearing dog placement officer, to check that all is going well and deal with any problems. Flint is also assessed on her response to the sounds I do not hear, such as the telephone, doorbell, smoke alarm and cooker timer.

 135

The charity started 21 years ago, and more than 1000 dogs have been placed with recipients all over the country. Some people are now with their second dog, and each one is as special to them as Flint is to me and my family.

Michael Sullivan
Kingswood, Bristol
England

In 2004, Flint was highly commended in the Life-Changing Hearing Dog of the Year award.

Lucy knew it was time to quit

I had been diagnosed with lung cancer, and lost a lung and my windpipe to surgery.

Doctors told me to wait two months before resuming my regular outdoor activities. We live in the country and heat our home with a wood-burning stove. I love splitting firewood with an axe, then stacking it into rows to be seasoned. When the doctors finally gave me the nod, I was off to the woodpile with axe in hand, and our dogs Lucy and Sugar came with me.

Sugar, a shepherd cross, is an excellent livestock dog. Lucy is a Catahoula leopard dog and not a good herder, although she is the larger of the two. Cattle run over her, and she runs along with horses as a game.

As I set to work chopping firewood, Lucy and Sugar found a sunny spot and lay down to nap. I began to tire after an hour or so, but kept saying to myself, 'Just one more chop and I'll quit.' I was becoming weak but thought, 'Just one more, just one more.'

Suddenly Lucy got up and blocked my way. She pressed her shoulder against my knee and wouldn't let me near the woodpile. She took my wrist gently in her mouth and began to pull me towards the house. I said, 'Lucy, just one more block to split', but she took the sleeve of my jacket in her teeth and again pulled me towards the house.

I put down the axe, smiled at her and said, 'Okay, you win.' When I started down the path to the house, Lucy let go of my sleeve and ran ahead, stopping often to make sure I was coming.

It doesn't matter that she's a poor livestock dog. She's in tune with me and takes care of me; it's as though she's my guardian angel.

Joan Manuliak
Lake Audy, Manitoba
Canada

How can we stop poor Ben's itch?

Recently my poor pug Ben got bitten on the bottom by a spider. According to the vet it wasn't a poisonous one, but it did leave a little cut. The cut healed nicely. However, his bottom is obviously still very itchy.

Ben now insists on rubbing his bottom on our shoes – while we're wearing them! This worries us, as sometimes it's quite embarrassing. The whole thing makes him quite sad too.

Can you offer any advice? Contact us at SMARTER than JACK.

The SMARTER than JACK story

We hope you've enjoyed this book. The SMARTER than JACK books are exciting and entertaining to create and so far we've raised over NZ$280,000 to help animals. We are thrilled!

Here's my story about how the SMARTER than JACK series came about.

Until late 1999 my life was a seemingly endless search for the elusive 'fulfilment'. I had this feeling that I was put on this earth to make a difference, but I had no idea how. Coupled with this, I had low self-confidence – not a good combination! This all left me feeling rather frustrated, lonely and unhappy with life. I'd always had a creative streak and loved animals. In my early years I spent many hours designing things such as horse saddles, covers and cat and dog beds. I even did a stint as a professional pet photographer.

Then I remembered something I was once told: do something for the right reasons and good things will come. So that's what I did. I set about starting Avocado Press and creating the first New Zealand edition in the SMARTER than JACK series. It was released in 2002 and all the profit went to the Royal New Zealand SPCA.

Good things did come. People were thrilled to be a part of the book and many were first-time writers. Readers were enthralled and many were delighted to receive the book as a gift from friends and family. The Royal New Zealand SPCA was over $43,000 better off and I received many encouraging letters and emails from readers and contributors. What could be better than that?

How could I stop there! It was as if I had created a living thing with the SMARTER than JACK series; it seemed to have a life all of its own. I now had the responsibility of evolving it. It had to continue to benefit animals and people by providing entertainment, warmth and something that people could feel part of. What an awesome responsibility and opportunity, albeit a bit of a scary one!

It is my vision to make SMARTER than JACK synonymous with smart animals, and a household name all over the world. The concept is already becoming well known as a unique and effective way for animal welfare charities to raise money, to encourage additional donors and to instil a greater respect for animals. The series is now in Australia, New Zealand, the United States, Canada and the United Kingdom.

Avocado Press, as you may have guessed, is a little different. We are about more than just creating books; we're about sharing information and experiences, and developing things in innovative ways. Ideas are most welcome too.

We feel it's possible to run a successful business that is both profitable and that contributes to animal welfare in a significant way. We want people to enjoy and talk about our books; that way, ideas are shared and the better it becomes for everyone.

Thank you for reading my story.

Jenny Campbell
Creator of SMARTER than JACK

Submit a story for our books

We are always creating more exciting books in the SMARTER than JACK series. Your true stories are continually being sought.

You can have a look at our website www.smarterthanjack.com. Here you can read stories, find information on how to submit stories, and read entertaining and interesting animal news. You can also sign up to receive the Story of the Week by email. We'd love to hear your ideas, too, on how to make the next books even better.

Guidelines for stories

- The story must be true and about a smart animal or animals.
- The story should be about 100 to 1000 words in length. We may edit it and you will be sent a copy to approve prior to publication.
- The story must be written from your point of view, not the animal's.
- Photographs and illustrations are welcome if they enhance the story, and if used will most likely appear in black and white.
- Submissions can be sent by post to SMARTER than JACK (see addresses on the following page) or via the website at www.smarterthanjack.com
- Include your name, postal and email address, and phone number, and indicate if you do not wish your name to be included with your story.
- Handwritten submissions are perfectly acceptable, but if you can type them, so much the better.
- Posted submissions will not be returned unless a stamped self-addressed envelope is provided.
- The writers of stories selected for publication will be notified prior to publication.
- Stories are welcome from everybody, and given the charitable nature of our projects there will be no prize money awarded, just recognition for successful submissions.

- Particpating animal welfare charities and Avocado Press have the right to publish extracts from the stories received without restriction of location or publication, provided the publication of those extracts helps promote the SMARTER than JACK series.

Where to send your story

Online
- Use the submission form at www.smarterthanjack.com or email it to submissions@smarterthanjack.com.

By post
- **In Australia**
  PO Box 170, Ferntree Gully, VIC 3156, Australia
- **In Canada and the United States**
  PO Box 819, Tottenham, ON, L0G 1W0, Canada
- **In New Zealand and rest of world**
  PO Box 27003, Wellington, New Zealand

Receive a free
SMARTER than JACK gift pack

Did you know that around half our customers buy the SMARTER than JACK books as gifts? We appreciate this and would like to thank and reward those who do so. If you buy eight books in the SMARTER than JACK series we will send you a free gift pack.

All you need to do is buy your eight books and either attach the receipt for each book or, if you ordered by mail, just write the date that you placed the order in one of the spaces on the next page. Then complete your details on the form, cut out the page and post it to us. We will then send you your SMARTER than JACK gift pack. Feel free to photocopy this form – that will save cutting a page out of the book.

Do you have a dog or a cat? You can choose from either a cat or dog gift pack. Just indicate your preference.

Note that the contents of the SMARTER than JACK gift pack will vary from country to country, but may include:

- The SMARTER than JACK mini Collector Series
- SMARTER than JACK postcards
- Soft animal toy
- Books in the SMARTER than JACK series

Show your purchases here:

Book 1	Book 2	Book 3	Book 4
Receipt attached ☐ *or* Date ordered _____	Receipt attached ☐ *or* Date ordered _____	Receipt attached ☐ *or* Date ordered _____	Receipt attached ☐ *or* Date ordered _____
Book 5	Book 6	Book 7	Book 8
Receipt attached ☐ *or* Date ordered _____	Receipt attached ☐ *or* Date ordered _____	Receipt attached ☐ *or* Date ordered _____	Receipt attached ☐ *or* Date ordered _____

Complete your details:

Your name: _____
Street address: _____
City/town: _____
State: _____
Postcode: _____
Country: _____
Phone: _____
Email: _____
Would you like a cat or dog gift pack?   CAT/DOG

Post the completed page to us:

- **In Australia**
  PO Box 170, Ferntree Gully, VIC 3156, Australia
- **In Canada and the United States**
  PO Box 819, Tottenham, ON, L0G 1W0, Canada
- **In New Zealand and rest of world**
  PO Box 27003, Wellington, New Zealand
Please allow four weeks for delivery.

Get more wonderful stories

Now you can receive a fantastic new-release SMARTER than JACK book every three months. That's a new book every March, June, September and December. The books are delivered to your door. It's easy!

Here's a sample of what you'd get if you signed up for four books over one year (option 2 on the order form) in September 2005:

- *Cats are SMARTER than JACK* in September 2005
- *Dogs are SMARTER than JACK* in December 2005
- *Heroic animals are SMARTER than JACK* in March 2006
- *Cheeky animals are SMARTER than JACK* in June 2006

Every time you get a book you will also receive a copy of *Smart Animals*, our members-only newsletter. Postage is included in the subscription price if the delivery address is in the United States, Canada, the United Kingdom, Australia or New Zealand.

You can also purchase existing titles in the SMARTER than JACK series. To purchase a book you can either go to your local bookstore or participating animal welfare charity, or order using the form at the end of the book.

How your purchase will help animals

The amount our partner animal welfare charities receive varies according to how the books are sold and the country in which they are sold. Contact your local participating animal welfare charity for more information.

In Australia

Smarter than Jack Limited is accepting orders on behalf of the RSPCA in Australia. Please send your order to:
SMARTER than JACK, PO Box 170, Ferntree Gully, VIC 3156

In Canada

The Canadian Federation of Humane Societies is accepting orders on behalf of the participating animal welfare charities in Canada, as listed below. Please send your order to:
CFHS, 102-30 Concourse Gate, Ottawa, ON, K2E 7V7

Please nominate from the following list the participating animal welfare charity that you would like to benefit from your book purchase:

- Alberta SPCA
- Bide A While Animal Shelter Society
- Calgary Humane Society
- Cochrane Humane Society
- Hamilton/Burlington SPCA
- Lakeland Humane Society
- Mae Bachur Animal Shelter
- Meadowlake and District Humane Society
- Newfoundland & Labrador SPCA
- Nova Scotia Humane Society
- Ontario SPCA
- Ottawa Humane Society
- PEI Humane Society
- Red Deer and District SPCA
- Saskatchewan SPCA
- SPA de l'Estrie
- Winnipeg Humane Society

In New Zealand

Please send your order to:
Royal New Zealand SPCA National Office, PO Box 15349, New Lynn, Auckland 1232

In the United Kingdom

Smarter than Jack Limited is accepting orders on behalf of the participating animal welfare charities in the United Kingdom, as listed below. Please send your order to:

SMARTER than JACK, FREEPOST NAT 11465, Northampton, NN3 6BR

Please nominate from the following list the participating animal welfare charity that you would like to benefit from your book purchase:

- Cats Protection
- Dogs Trust

In the United States

Smarter than Jack Limited is accepting orders on behalf of the participating animal welfare charities in the United States, as listed below. Please send your order to:

SMARTER than JACK, 45 High Street N, Thunder Bay, ON, P7A 5R1, CANADA

Please nominate from the following list the participating animal welfare charity that you would like to benefit from your book purchase:

- Alley Cat Allies
- American Humane Association
- Animal Rescue Foundation Inc.
- Cat Care Society
- Feral Friends Animal Rescue and Assistance
- Humane Society of Lewisville
- Jeff Davis County Humane Society
- People for the Ethical Treatment of Animals (PETA)
- Pets911
- West Plains Regional Animal Shelter

Rest of world

Please send your order to:
SMARTER than JACK, PO Box 27003, Wellington,
NEW ZEALAND

Purchase from your local bookstore

Your local bookstore should have the editions you want or, if not, be able
to order them for you. If they can't get the books, the publisher Avocado
Press can be contacted direct:
By email: orders@smarterthanjack.com
By post: Avocado Press Limited, PO Box 27003, Wellington,
NEW ZEALAND

Order online

To order online go to www.supportanimals.com

How much are the books?

* Australia $19.95
* Canada $17.95 plus taxes
* New Zealand $19.95
* United Kingdom £7.99
* United States $11.95 plus taxes

Order form

What books would you like?

A new-release book every three months The books are sent out in March, June, September and December. You will receive your first book in the appropriate month after we receive your order.	Quantity	Total
Option 1: two books over six months	2	
Option 2: four books over one year	4	
Option 3: eight books over two years	8	
Existing books in the series		
Animals are SMARTER than JACK (2005) *Canada and the USA only*		
Cats are SMARTER than JACK (2005)		
Dogs are SMARTER than JACK (2005)		
Australian animals are SMARTER than JACK 1 (2003) *Australia only*		
Australian animals are SMARTER than JACK 2 (2004) *Australia only*		
Canadian animals are SMARTER than JACK 1 (2004) *Canada only*		
Why animals are SMARTER than US (2004) *Australia, New Zealand, Canada and the USA only*		
Applicable taxes		
Subtotal for order		
Packaging and post: for orders of existing books only, please add $5 or £2		
Total		

For Canada, United States and United Kingdom orders only – using the lists on the preceding pages, please indicate which animal welfare charity in your country you would like to benefit from your order:

_____

Choose the payment method

There are two ways you can pay:

- By cheque/check/postal order made out to the organisation you are sending it to and posted, along with your completed order form, to one of the addresses listed or
- Fill in the credit card details below:

Card type: Visa/Mastercard

Card number: ☐☐☐☐ ☐☐☐☐ ☐☐☐☐ ☐☐☐☐ ☐☐☐☐

Name on card: _____   Expiry date: _____

Complete your details

Your name: _____

Street address: _____

City/town: _____

State: _____

Postcode: _____

Country: _____

Phone: _____

Email: _____

Send in your order

Post your order to your nearest participating animal welfare charity or Smarter than Jack Limited at one of the addresses listed on pages 146–148, according to which country you live in.

Please note that some of the books are only available in certain countries.